not drowning, reading

Despite a reading and writing disability in childhood, Andrew Relph understood that reading was fundamental to his emotional survival, and that in literature lay his consolation and salvation.

This extraordinary series of essays reveals a life via the books the author has encountered, and shows how one might chart a course through reading.

From Amis to Bellow, Blake to Gallico, and Shakespeare to Woolf, these essays ask why it is that our relationships with authors and their characters can be as valuable as any we form in 'real life'.

This is a memoir about the art, and the gift, of reading.

about the author

Andrew Relph is a clinical psychologist and psychotherapist who lives and works in Perth. *Not Drowning, Reading* is his first book.

Book club notes available from
www.fremantlepress.com.au

not drowning, reading

andrew relph

For the desire to read, like all the other desires which distract our unhappy souls, is capable of analysis.
  – Virginia Woolf, 'Sir Thomas Browne'

I see Bellow perhaps twice a year, and we call and we write. But that accounts for only a fraction of the time I spend in his company. He is on the shelves, on the desk, he is all over the house, and always in the mood to talk. That's what writing is, not communication but a means of communion. And here are the other writers who swirl around you, like friends, patient, intimate, sleeplessly accessible, over centuries. This is the definition of literature.
  – Martin Amis, *Experience*

*For those who have helped to read me.
The authors, the lovers and friends,
the psychotherapists and clients, and the editor.
And now you.*

contents

Prelude	1
The stolen child	10
Sally and Miriam	21
Shopping with Clara	30
Reading and writing	39
Intermezzo	50
Ignoring Icarus	62
Did you read *Doctor Zhivago*?	71
Hamlet	87
My mother's book	102
Being Herzog	114
Brothers and fathers	132
The space in the story	146
Coda	160
Sources	166
Acknowledgements	173

prelude

I

Drops of rain collect over the southern English countryside. They form rivulets down little banks. Small clear-water springs ooze up from behind muddy shale. Brooks a foot wide make little conversational sounds. Here are streams you can wade across. Here livestock slake their thirst in long sucking draughts. Here are small rivers deep enough to take a rowing boat to fish for grayling in the morning light. Meandering with gravitas nearer the sea, the river's pale blue sheen and appearance of resting gently on the rich meadowlands belies its power to inundate the countryside when the shoal at the mouth builds with the longshore drift of the English Channel.

When is a river deep enough to drown in? The River Ouse was deep enough, evidently, on that early spring morning when Virginia realised there was no way out from her madness and assumed that Leonard and the world would be better off without her. Yet her choice of death was more poetic than hostile. It seemed that she had always let nature in too strongly; there was too thin a membrane between her and the apprehension of existence. Now she only needed pebbles in the pockets of her dress to hold her to the bottom of that cool river. To let nature overwhelm her, decisively, insensitively – little drops of nature which, just then, no longer provided for life but took it away.

When I first picked up a book for myself I couldn't master the element of words and, if I'd known how difficult that skill would be to acquire, I would have gone under. As it was, I chose a book that my mother would read aloud to me, that daily activity which nurtured my early imagination. In my youth I was first disheartened, then challenged, by the difficulty of reading; I swam against the intimidation of books with a slow and plucky dog-paddle until I got my degree.

Thirty-five years later came another kind of intimidation: not of learning to read but of encountering the great mass of books in the university library. I felt the overwhelming nature of the words on the page and the pages in all the volumes on the three levels of that large building. I could drown in so many words. This thought filled me not with the panic of my childhood, more a sense that one day I would sink below the surface of all that literature and disappear into it. The stuff that had nurtured me, the stuff that had kept me alive, would one day be a place in which I would submerge entirely.

There were two statements about beginning I recalled from the Bible, the book I heard repeated most as a young child.

The first was in Genesis:

In the beginning God created the heaven and the earth. And the earth was without form and void; and darkness was on the face of the deep. And the Spirit of God moved upon the face of the waters.

Water, dark water, deep water – dark and elemental expanses before the first sunrise, after the last sunset. A question hanging over the whole of existence. It made my head swirl, my young head, my beginning head, void and without form.

The second statement was at the start of The Gospel According to St John: *In the beginning was the Word, and the Word was with God, and the Word was God.* That had always seemed to me a curiously advanced place to begin the history of Christianity. That was until I realised that life, with its beginning described in Genesis, led to *consciousness* and that it was all those words which enabled the next great step: relationship – secular or sacred. When I was read to as a child, I knew at some level that I was in relationship, though I would have been unsure whether that was mostly the feeling between me and my mother or between me and the character in the book. When finally I could read on my own, it was the characters rather than the author I felt related to. The words constructed the characters, who offered me a connection to the world, and began to help me create myself. There were books to be read at school but I resisted other people's ideas. I sensed that my parents and teachers knew little of what I needed and I was vigilant against the criticism and humiliation which often attended my attempts at reading and writing. In spite of this, some books made an impression in those years, the story and the language slipping past the deep suspicion I had of teachers to appeal directly to me.

Only later, at university, did I imagine the deep connection between me and the author. Although I was largely unconscious of what I might be getting out of the process, I found myself systematically engaging with literature. This was not a random process but one based on the curriculum of the English department. By doing this, and without realising it, I had started on the long process, via relationship, of my identity development. I rushed into relationship with Lawrence and George Eliot, Conrad and Austen, in a way which had seemed impossible with the live adult models of my childhood. Where there had been resistance and rebellion there was now consolation and identity. I was ready to read with a force of purpose which others, who perhaps have related more closely to family and school in childhood, or who have read with more ease, do not feel.

Perhaps the trust which some people establish early in life leaves them able to interact in a less defensive way. Within the embrace of a close family, unthreatening to survival, one might be able to read an identity for oneself forged from direct relationships. Perhaps some people love reading but don't *require* it.

II

Once I came very close to drowning. I did not mean to drown but, if I had, it's possible some people would have thought it suicide. A young man who has seen a psychiatrist is a vulnerable narrative. People might have said I was unhappy; might have said I was on pills to help me cope – with goodness knows what. A strange family, people might have said. A father who was distant and shook his son's hand as a sign of affection when he returned home for the university holidays. A mother who was easily sick and who made those close to her sick: a nurse-mother with the currency of illness. Pills and psychiatrists suited her as they did not so readily suit me.

At that stage, university staff knew I was studying the interpersonal complexities of D.H. Lawrence. They quipped in the English department that my project may have been mistakenly handed in to the psychology department if it was picked up on the lawn outside the library. My tutor, with his sharp sensitivity, may even have drawn a connection to the drowning in *Women in Love: Why come to life again? There's room under that water there for thousands.* There had been thousands of moments by then when nature could have overwhelmed me. I came so close to staying below the thin line of the surface, giving up and, dead to literature, losing the solace it offered.

We had been paddling a two-man canoe in the middle of the four-hundred-acre dam on the outskirts of the town. We had tipped up in our uncoordinated enthusiasm and could not right the boat. Taking responsibility for swimming the boat to shore, my friend set out immediately. I could have called out to him then: 'Wait, I don't think I can make it from here.' But I did not. It was a matter of judgement and I made an error.

Nigel was a self-possessed twenty year old agriculture student. He struck out for the closest bank and did not look behind him until three-quarters of the way to the shore. If he had turned minutes earlier he would have seen me waving my arms and calling against the wind. But now he saw what he thought was his friend making slow but deliberate progress through the water. He only thought how far behind I was, not that I might be in difficulty. He could not see me gulp for air, or take in another mouthful of silty, bad-smelling water, my arms weighed down, my feet dangling at sixty degrees in the murk.

When he reached the shore Nigel pulled himself and the boat out of the water. He collapsed face-first, his chest pushing out underneath him onto the coarse warm sand. After a few minutes he rolled onto his back; a few more and he propped his head up in his cupped hands to look at the water-horizon. Shit, where was his friend?

I do not know how I made it through the last hundred metres of water. Nigel had started emptying the canoe to come and get me, but by the time he was ready to launch it, my feet had touched the muddy bottom and I had dragged my body out myself, twice falling facedown in the water in the last twenty metres. My survival that afternoon was never talked about between us, nor did I tell anyone else about it. The whole experience was covered in a shroud of shame which I did not understand.

Unlike me, Nigel had no need for novels. He spent his idle moments lying on his bed reading popular science magazines alongside his girlfriend, who read girls' magazines about orgasms and food, but had little of either. Nigel liked camping in the mountains more than he liked reading. I, on the other hand, learned from an early age that to read was to survive. The consolation of literature gave me buoyancy.

I wonder now whether I can convey this strange way I have had of constructing my identity, by giving you an account of my interaction with the books I have read and the meaning they have made of me. How, with this meaning, I have become a psychotherapist and spend my days in conversation with people struggling to give definition to who they are becoming. What is the self-defining conversation which flows through reading as it does through other relationships? Let me tell you my case, while you bring yours to what I have written.

Like Nigel, the other person I never knew to read a novel was my father. The newspaper, especially the financial pages, seemed to entertain him. He told me once that he had read Charles Kingsley's *Westward Ho!* when he was a young man and that it had a great influence on him. Late in life he had a nameplate made for his new house, brass with cursive black letters, which he had mounted on the pillar at the front gate. There was, by then, no one but him and his new wife living in the large modern house with extensive gardens. He longed for his adult children to visit and even fantasised about our mother visiting him after their years apart. He was proud of his new house; if his parents had been alive he'd have liked to show it off to them. He called it Westward Ho! That was the extent of the literary influence in his life.

When I read Martin Amis' autobiographical account of his family and particularly of his father, I could not think of a person who would have been less like my own father than Kingsley Amis. Although in many ways just as difficult a character as my father, at least he read and wrote. What refreshment might come, I thought, from having a father like that. Imagine a mother, a father, any family member, who spoke the same language as me. If that had been the case I might never have been propelled into such crucial, life-saving reading. Reading could instead have been a pasttime for me as it was for so many people – like swimming for pleasure not survival.

But just as I could not read easily when most I would have benefited from the facility, so too some of what I have read came later than a time I could have fully used it. Take Milan Kundera. It was only after I had flown the communist-phobic Stalinist state of my adolescence that I finally roused Kundera from where, to me, he had been sleeping on the shelves. Perhaps he had been banned in my homeland. What he had to tell me and the questions he had to ask me about my emerging political consciousness in South Africa were silent until I was already liberated into a greater freedom and an enlarged perspective in Australia. Kundera showed me where I had been, though that was consolation itself. He showed me, also too late, what I had needed to know in my twenties and thirties about the difference between men and women. When I read *The Joke*, Kundera would have appreciated that history was enjoying a good laugh, the book coming to me twenty years too late.

When is a river deep enough to drown in? Who is lost and who is saved? The hand that filled the pockets with pebbles created images which still make the reader pause in recognition: they wrench, then soothe, then unsettle anew. Strange that others can find her still, when she lost herself.

We know there was consolation for *her* in reading. She would need no reward in heaven, she once wrote, being one of the company that had loved reading. Did reading eventually fail her? She had reached out and touched the anguished Hardy and the soothing Gray. Was there insufficient salve for her despair in Wordsworth, whose letters she termed her only drug? Perhaps those who had loved reading and who, in writing, had left their mark on it, had done what they could for her. Perhaps without them she may not have stayed so long.

the stolen child

Come away, O human child!
To the waters and the wild
With a faery, hand in hand,
For the world's more full of weeping than you can understand.
– W.B. Yeats, 'The Stolen Child'

I

Ireland. Here lay the consolation of the land itself. I had always somehow known that in this place the very soil would be sympathetic.

The Dingle Peninsula is approached from across the water. It is first sighted by the visitor approaching from the south-east across the broad bay of the same name. Through mist or driving rain, the late afternoon sunlight can make the finger of land stretching out towards America appear as in a dream. So it was, that late September day. I saw it through the windscreen wipers, through the rain, and through sunlight that reflected sharply off the ocean. Through the thousand shimmering tears, I saw the low green hills, dreamlike, suspended between grey sky and grey ocean.

The town was small and banked up on the bay as if it had been washed there by a particularly high tide. By the time we had explored the harbour, the rain had stopped and darkness had begun to settle quietly over the strand. The buildings of the town were losing their colour and the lights were coming on. The house where we would stay was barely fifteen minutes drive away. First we would have dinner in town.

The restaurant was yellow with light and noisy with people as we entered. I was dimly aware of the protest contained in the signs and menus that were written in Irish. I asked the waiter about it and she said that in this settlement the official language was Irish. English, it seemed, was tolerated.

In the black night, we navigated the four miles to the house. It was illuminated only by the dim light over the front door. To me it was unexpectedly modern in its construction. The tourist office in Dublin had said it was on castle lands and I had impulsively asked them to book a room. Shown upstairs with our heavy suitcases, we were soon in bed; weary travellers with a day full of sensations. When the lights were out, I lay on my back retracing our journey. It was a night when the air itself seemed black.

Four hours later I awoke from a dream and everything had changed. The curtains were illuminated from without. The careless gap between the drapes sent a skein of colourless light across the end of the bed. I pulled myself up on my elbows, orienting myself. Ireland, yes; Dingle, yes; the bed and breakfast. And the light? Unmistakably the full moon at its zenith. My chest and scalp felt swollen and tingling with sensation. I had become sharply awake, as if primitively I knew instant action was required. I sat peering from the headboard, arrested by the moonlight on the mountain peaks of my feet and, next to me, the sleeping form of my companion. My body was oddly still, in comparison to my mind, which urgently clung first to the emotion and then to the images from which I'd woken.

I had been at the base of a medieval scaffolding set up to execute people. Hanging or burning perhaps. A large wooden tower formed the centre of the platform and, around this, with their hands linked together, were women. Were they chained together? Yes, chained. Their hands? No, their waists, where their dresses narrowed then bulged. They were holding hands as in a country dance in an outward facing circle. (Had I, sometime before, seen a clock-tower contraption that played a tune on the hour with a miniature stage on which country women danced in an outward facing circle, smiling?) In the dream, it seemed there were two or three ranks of women arranged around the central post. They looked out to where I watched, in a crowd of onlookers. They were not smiling; they were crying.

This scene of grief was vivid. In my ears still was a sound of unbearable pain. The women were wailing, plaintive and beautiful; almost sweetly. As they wept, they rocked backwards and forwards slowly with each other and with the sound. I tried to recapture the words. Strange words, ancient Irish words. Surprised, I realised I had understood them. They were crying for the lost people. *'It's you, it's you must go and I must bide.'* The children, the young soldiers, the women in childbirth, the starved, the revolutionaries, the alcoholics. The collective grief was swelling and dying. Tears were falling onto the soil at my feet and the air was full of sadness. Now I was shaking and rocking on the bed and the weeping was now in my chest. The words were in my head: something must be done about the grief of the Irish people.

Something must be done about my grief.

The floor was cold on my feet as I walked across the room and with both hands parted the curtains. Opening the double windows with the single catch, I looked out onto the ruins of a small castle less than fifty metres away. We had not seen it in the darkness of our arrival. Now, the light was bright and the night was terribly quiet. The moss-covered walls were irregularly decayed, the masonry seemed to be resisting being taken back into the earth. All around, stretching out on the low hills and down to the ocean, the air was cool and sad. It lay like a mantle of moonlit mourning. I was conscious of it lying across many generations. This was cultural despair; here was a geographic grief. I could feel in myself a merging sympathy. Was that in my chest or was it in the air? I stood unclothed, brave in the night air as one can be when one is still warm from bed. There, breathing in the night light, entranced by the vision of the ruin I'd not seen before, and still straining to hear the dregs of the sad singing, I began to experience the relief that comes from shared and recognised pain.

This was a beginning; the start of consolation.

To take back that weeping child who had been stolen. To resist the longed-for comfort of others: the women who would cry for me; the land that would be green and soaked with tears; and the people who would sing sad songs for the child who would never be soothed. Let the aching subside rather than have it define me. Take back my own childhood and care for it myself. True consolation is internal. True consolation takes courage and responsibility. Only now, accepting this responsibility, could I understand that the source of my sadness was not only the unresponsiveness of those who had cared for me as a child. There was a deeper well of grief that was not mine; it was my mother's I'd spent my life experiencing for her. It had happened because she had neglected her grief and, in the moment of greatest pain shied away.

II

I had garnered the story from my reluctant parents. It was the year before I was born that Howard had got sick. My mother had been a nurse; she'd interrupted her training to marry my father. Together they had three healthy children in quick succession. Gifts from God, they said. They had joked about the first two boys; the first was hers and the second, his. The girl that came next seemed strangely to belong to neither of them, at least not as strongly as the boys.

Howard, the second boy, died a little after his second

birthday. It was so quick that no one could comprehend what had happened.

In the morning he was playing happily with his brother. They had a spot in the dirt, at the side of the house, where they spent time with blocks of wood and buckets and trikes. In the afternoon, Howard was suddenly sick, very sick, and she'd taken him to the doctor. Yes, he had a high temperature and seemed to be in pain. It was Saturday, specialists were difficult to get hold of and the hospital would mean a long wait; it would be uncomfortable for them both. Why not take him home, tepid sponge him? She'd learnt how to do that in nursing college; keep an eye on him till tomorrow.

Tomorrow he was dead. He had worsened during the night and become weak. My father said he'd got up to the little boy in that darkest of nights and seen his life was draining away. They'd driven him to the hospital and within half an hour the doctor had come out with the terrible news. Fifteen hours before, he'd had his last go on his little blue trike. It was still there, abandoned in the driveway.

The day of the funeral she was composed and distant. After the ceremony she told her husband and her mother that the Lord had spoken to her. He had taken little Howard to be his servant. He would be an angel in the heavenly realm. His purpose would be greater than any earthly purpose. She must not be sad; she must open her hands to God and let her child go.

In the weeks that followed, my father emerged out of the shock into a terrible grief which, from time to time for the rest of his life, would overwhelm him. At the same time, my mother found inspiration in religion. She told her husband over and over, as if reading from a shopping list, it had been God's will that little Howard had been taken from them. As she glowed with this sacrifice, her grief was aborted. In her prayers she whispered that she identified with Mary and the loss of her son to God for the fulfilment of a wonderful plan. She sang hymns of praise, while my father could not listen to 'Danny Boy' without leaving the room, his face congested with unacknowledged tears. He could not bear the loneliness of his own grief. He could not yet allow himself the violent anger he felt in response to these strange and distant ideas into which his wife had fallen.

But God had not taken her grief away. She had fiercely excised it from her heart and refused to let it into her thoughts. Everyone seemed to idolise her for her Christian virtue. Wasn't it wonderful she could hand her grief over to God? In fact, she'd handed it over to a magical new life stirring within her. I had come to be conceived in this strange climate of grief, anger and religious perversion.

When another boy was born, my father's grief was partly assuaged. 'He can be a replacement for our little Howardie,' he said. But her distant smile conveyed to him, as it always did, a kind of absence. Something had always been missing for her. It had made in her a deep detachment which, while felt by those close by, was seldom seen by others.

Yet, there was genuine excitement in her voice one evening when my father came in from work. 'He's got a God-given gift,' she said, and he was pleased that she'd found something to love in the infant whose eyes always were looking, searching. 'Yes,' she said, 'this morning I had the terrible pain again. I was lying down. He started crying in his crib. I picked him up and held him above me and his feet touched my sternum where the pain was greatest. It was miraculous, do you understand? His feet were hot, really hot, and as they touched me the pain vanished. I think he's got healing feet!' Though taken aback, my father was outwardly enthusiastic. But his mind went darkly to his lost love, his son. For my mother, my dandling feet were truly a gift. The pain was in her chest. It was the only manifestation of the grief she could not bear. But, for the young boy, it became my burden. My mother's grief became my grief. It was why I watched her so carefully. I was looking for something that had no outward sign.

III

A great tide had been held back. A powerful wall had been erected, buttressed by the pronouncements of God himself. When, as a young child, I first began to experience emotion I could feel it sweeping over me, inundating me with unreasoning sadness. Nor could this strange inner force be understood or contained in the usual ways of parenting.

Sleeping during daylight was particularly bad for me as a child. That little death, which some people develop a liking for, became, later, something to be avoided. Tiredness overcame me easily; and I would go to sleep, but when I awoke I would be covered with despair. I would run wildly, tears coursing down my face, to my mother and spend several minutes sobbing, my face buried in her skirt. It was fortunate I had no inkling then that she, the comforter, was the source of this emotional tumult. Children are pragmatic, as all animals are; I simply learnt never to sleep during the day.

Recognising the sadness in me created a sort of bond between mother and son. When she realised I loved being read to, she did so frequently but often from books which nurtured my unhappiness. She would read, I would cry, and she could experience in *me* what she could not in herself.

My memories of the daily events of my childhood are much less full and fluent than of the stories that she read me. I cannot recall whether I lay next to her or sat at her feet. My experience was not of the top half of her body. I cannot recall if she wore glasses. I especially cannot recall what she did with my tears when the story became too sad for me. But I do know that she continued to read, and often the stories were sad. Did she select sad stories to read to me or have I selected them from the stories we shared?

I remember *The Snow Goose*. My mother first read me Paul Gallico's story when I was eight or nine. She may have read it to me again later. My child's mind wanted the same things repeated; and there was, now I recall, a vinyl record that dramatised the story and which I wept to hear whenever I played it to myself. Later, as a young adult, I read the story again. What was it that so captured my mind? I can still see and smell the saltmarshes where the disfigured man lived, away from people, in the abandoned lighthouse. I can still picture Rhayader the man and Frith the girl who brought to him the injured snow goose. Most of all I can see, not so much in memory, but as a part of me, the large white bird with black wingtips. I see her soaring upwards as she takes to the sky after her wing mended, dwarfing the figures on the ground. I don't have to read it now to remember the words that passed between them:

'Look! Look! The Princess! Be she going away?'
    Rhayader stared into the sky at the climbing specks. 'Ay,' he said, unconsciously dropping into her manner of speech. 'The Princess is going home. Listen! she is bidding us farewell.'

This scene, and the two people, defined me. The big-breasted bird, soaring, defined me. This was not a daydream stimulated by some pattern in the curtains of my bedroom. Here, I was entering a world, fully formed. It seemed more vivid than the room where I sat or the suburb where I lived. I now realise how much I longed to be somewhere else and how my mind's eye was, even then, more real than the world around me. But there was another reason why this story had me in its thrall. I was learning about emotions. Those associated with the bonds between people gripped my young heart and hurt it again and again. People? Yes, and animals. I made no distinction between my family and my dog, the birds in the aviary, and the two tortoises. So, Frith's and Rhayader's connection to the Princess and how that connected them to each other and to the world of suffering, was instantly recognisable to me. I was Frith's age. The love, and with it the pain, of the unfolding drama between the goose, the man, the girl and the world at war, gave me connection. The story didn't cause me such waves of grief and sadness so much as it allowed me their expression.

What had I lost? What death in my family? What war? At the time I was puzzled as I drifted in the misery unable to disentangle the sadness or liberate personal from historical grief. None of it was explicit. The minister on Sundays would have seen a regular sort of family; but I was going home to play the record of *The Snow Goose* again, and to look out of the window and up into the grey sky and let the tears run ceaselessly down my cheeks.

sally and miriam

When we are young, and read most passionately and repeatedly, we are likely to identify, perhaps somewhat naively, with favourite characters in a novel. As I observed in regard to Mann's The Magic Mountain, *such pleasure of identification is a legitimate part of the reading experience, at any age, even if such pleasure passes, in middle age and later, from naive to sentimental ... Characters meet other characters as we meet new persons, open to the disorders of discovery, and we need to be open to what we read, in a parallel way.*

– Harold Bloom, *How to Read and Why*

She was full and generous and confident. She was much more certain about almost everything than I was. Her name was Sally and she was my first real girlfriend. Her young heart was easily moved to sympathy; when it was, the flicker of mockery in her smiling eyes would disappear. At other times it would flare up into a haughty and condescending laugh. I was never sure which she would give me: a lover's understanding hand on my forearm or a shove in the back as if from a smirking sibling. Sally's mother was so soft she was hardly there at all. Her father by contrast was an opinionated, at times cantankerous, man. The humours were blended in Sally who loved both of them more dearly than I'd seen parents appreciated before. Keith said that in the British Army (it was never clear how long he'd actually spent there), there were standards. When you polished your shoes, for example, you would not neglect to shine the bit of unscuffed leather which lies between the heel and the pad of the sole, the part that doesn't touch the ground. He held out his leg from his chair as if ready for inspection. He had a way of half-closing one eye with a smile and then making a pronouncement from off-centre of his moustached mouth. He made a lot of these statements to me – the son he never had – over a tumbler of whisky.

When I came to the audition for the play Keith was directing, he cast me in the leading role the same night. I could act, and a bit of grease paint would cover up the acne that marred my unusual face. By the end of the evening he'd introduced me to Sally who, he said, was helping out backstage and would be our prompt when it came to the performances. He also asked me to come to Sunday lunch with his family the next weekend. Soon after, he pointed out his collection of Chopin records to me and said I could play them whenever I liked. Keith admitted me into his family, and then Sally and I fell in love with each other, brother and sister, with Keith overseeing things. It suited me. No one in my family had ever acted. No one would have understood the erotic feeling I got when I dressed up backstage as a primary school student ready for my entrance in *A Christmas Carol*.

No one would have understood the powerful pleasure of an audience responding from behind the harsh lights which enlivened my sense of the fitted identity. No one in my family listened to Chopin. But Keith understood and so did Sally. To my surprise and joy she seemed to understand nearly everything I said to her. She was sixteen, I was seventeen: my parents were in the final stages of a three-year violent and acrimonious break-up; Sally's parents looked like they would be together forever, and as far as I know they were.

I soon realised that, though I was surrounded by the first pleasures of an understanding touch from another, and though her family had given me a rare feeling of familiarity, I was seldom unambiguously happy in Sally's presence. There was a companion of dissatisfaction with me, a sadness which would materialise first in the thought of another person, then in the idea of another relationship. I had always imagined an unambiguous love and, for a time, that was Sally. I wanted nothing more than to make love to her, though she resisted moralistically. I wanted to be with her forever, but as she cared for me and protected me, as she made me feel safe, there grew, twined with my love, the possibility of separation. That safety bred a kind of hopefulness about the world, a braveness which might make other possibilities real.

Then I met Lyle, a girl who I thought had the most sympathetic eyes I had ever seen and the most sympathetic voice I had ever heard. Now I wanted to be with her. One night there was a party at my house with my friends; Sally and Lyle were both there. Lyle had some temporary bad temper so I drove her home early and said we'd patch it up sometime soon. Then I hurried back home to find Sally who was happy and wanting to have a good time. I grew to realise how difficult it was to sustain myself in the face of a woman's bad mood. Had I caused the bad feeling? My impulse was to get away. But I didn't want to get away to be on my own, I wanted to be with someone who would reassure me, tell me I was wanted, tell me I'd done nothing wrong. And as soon as I received any sign of reassurance, I would be unable to stay. Happy again, charged with a new hope, I would want to return to the woman who was at the centre of my life. So it was: one woman at the centre and one woman on the edge. Each sustaining my relationship with the other.

I must have understood this pattern even before Sally. Looking back, it was deeply part of my family, my early relationship with my parents and their relationship with each other – a relationship DNA. I certainly recognised the pattern with a sense of familiarity when I read *Sons and Lovers* the same year as I met Sally.

Lyle was not the first Miriam in my life – the girl who, in her beauty, has both sensitivity and sympathy. Like a dark secret, I discovered in childhood that I could imagine such sentiments in complete strangers. Once, when I was six or seven, I built a sandcastle on the beach with a dark-haired girl of my own age. It was a perfect spring afternoon and she seemed to me perfect in every way. Though she was unknown to me or my family and though I only spent an hour or two in her company, I could bring her to my imagination for years afterwards. There were many such encounters with the sympathetic girl. I would pass her in a shopping centre or see her from the window of a car or dine with her in a restaurant a few tables away.

This Miriam-like woman was so much a part of me that I recognised her instantly in Lawrence's descriptions, brushing aside any slight misalignment with the woman in my imagination.

> One day in March he lay on the bank of Nethermere, with Miriam sitting beside him. It was a glistening, white-and-blue day. Big clouds, so brilliant, went by overhead, while shadows stole along on the water. The clear spaces in the sky were of clean, cold blue. Paul lay on his back in the old grass, looking up. He could not bear to look at Miriam. She seemed to want him, and he resisted. He resisted all the time. He wanted now to give her passion and tenderness, and he could not. He felt that she wanted the soul out of his body, and not him. All his strength and energy she drew into herself through some channel which united them. She did not want to meet him, so that there were two of them, man and woman together. She wanted to draw all of him into her. It urged him to an intensity like madness, which fascinated him, as drug-taking might.

Unlike the troubled protagonist of *Sons and Lovers*, I imagined that when confronted by the woman of such intensity, I would not resist her desperate wish for unity however costly it may be for me. I would willingly sacrifice myself on the pyre of our intensity; disappear where I had hardly yet made an appearance. It would take me half a life to discover how this might be done without self-destruction. Half a life to feel again the innocence of merging, yet this time from a solid position of my own. Where William Blake's 'innocence regained through experience' would not find relevance in me for another twenty years, Lawrence gave me something for that developmental moment. In those adolescent days all I knew is what I longed for, not how it might be achieved.

As far as I knew, neither Sally nor Lyle read much. From time to time I would recite lines to them from the books I was reading. The intensity with which I had received the writing seemed to fascinate them more than any wish to read themselves.

Just as Lyle was not the only Miriam, Sally was not the only Clara in my life.

> *She had scornful grey eyes, a skin like white honey, and a full mouth, with a slightly lifted upper lip that did not know whether it was raised in scorn of all men or out of eagerness to be kissed, but which believed the former. She carried her head back, as if she had drawn away in contempt, perhaps from men also.*

Like Lara in *Dr Zhivago* (the sameness of their names only now arrests me) these are married women, unhappily so, and the rivalry is with the man who one can best.

Yet it was more than a recognition of the two women in *Sons and Lovers* which drew me in to reading Lawrence. It was the depiction of the battles which ensued when the adolescent man, coming away from an overwhelming yet unsatisfactory relationship with a mother, who herself has an unhappy and unsatisfying relationship with her husband, tries to move into the world. Clara and Miriam are representative, archetypal, yet it was the action between them and Paul – suffocating in his relationship with his mother – which I recognised with deep connection but dim awareness.

To relate to Miriam with all her suffering tenderness and capacity to enflame such passionate intensity, to bring out the artist and the musician in the man, Paul will have to leave his mother and find a space in his realised adult identity for this passion. It is his mother that the young man transgresses with in his relationship with Miriam, a first psychological step towards real independence which in relationships is so often aborted. But with Clara it is not away from the mother; she *is* the mother, a much more satisfying mother – and the boy, now suddenly catapulted into manhood, satisfies her with his sensitivity where her lover has failed.

It feels now as though my awareness of this pattern when I first read *Sons and Lovers* was like the awareness I had when I first played the piano. I was six or seven before I ever had lessons. Before that, some notes sounded good together, others did not; a pattern existed which I could use to make my otherwise random sounds more pleasing. I knew that a pattern existed but I had little understanding of it.

Similarly when Sally appeared to lose interest in me, I would have accounted for it, too simply, in the same way as I understood Clara's willingness to dispense with her relationship with Paul – she somehow didn't like him any more. But the literature pushed me to an analysis of the protagonists which I was not ready for in my own life. Clara's action in breaking off with Paul is predicated on her assessment that he is still emotionally with his mother and therefore unavailable to her, to Miriam, or to anyone else. One could say I wasn't aware of that pattern in myself until many years later when I could look back and see that my understanding of it had its beginning in that early reading of Lawrence. In my forties I had a fuller realisation of this pattern which I documented in a piece called 'Shopping with Clara' about my relationship with a woman in which those features at last were recognised during, not after, the relationship.

Awake and writing; not in a dream and reading.

At nineteen I would have liked to write a naive and self-indulgent letter to Lawrence explaining what resonance I felt, not just with Paul, but with the women in his life. How he'd shed light on my feelings for women and made a continuity between that and the landscape. Just as I noticed the natural environment of Johannesburg differently after the descriptions of Nottinghamshire, so after reading Lawrence I noticed my relationships differently. How the passion went out of the sky as Paul and Miriam watched the sunset. How the author consoled me also, in my perceived deprivation, with many descriptions of industrial poverty which I had felt in other ways. And how he'd introduced the idea that an interest in books and painting, though stimulated by the women in one's life, was a doorway to the creation of one's own aesthetic, shaken free from the dictates of those women.

Instead, I chose to move on from *Sons and Lovers* to *The Rainbow* and to *Women in Love*, to the short stories and *Lady Chatterley's Lover* – in fact, all the Lawrence I could get my hands on. And then to write an essay for the English department defending Lawrence's characters from the criticisms, famously launched at them, that they were unreal. This was a much more sound and disciplined exercise than the letter. I think it was then that I began to think of my reading as a direct relationship with Lawrence, then that I began to get the idea of the relationship between author and reader transcending that of reader and narrative.

On the simplest level though, I did feel like Paul in relation to Sally and Lyle and my mother, and so, reading about him and the characters in the ensuing novels could be said to be a form of psychotherapy, a psychodrama. Novels and the characters within them were commenting on my life, especially my interpersonal life, in much the same way as, later, psychotherapy would do.

And so, like relationships past, I value Lawrence still, and keep *Sons and Lovers* at the centre of the shelf in the bookcase where those most deeply connected to me reside. There, like Lyle and Sally, the influence continues, though the relationship is now unpractised and not pertinent to this passage of my life. I look back on my reading with questions more than judgements about that part which reading played in my emergence from the scenery and crowd of extras, with slow long acts and many set changes, to take at last, the lead role in my life.

shopping with clara

'Where should we go for dinner?' asked the mother.
    It was felt to be a reckless extravagance. Paul had only been in an eating-house once or twice in his life, and then only to have a cup of tea and a bun … Real cooked dinner was considered great extravagance. Paul felt rather guilty.
    They found a place that looked quite cheap. But when Mrs. Morel scanned the bill of fare, her heart was heavy, things were so dear. So she ordered kidney pies and potatoes as the cheapest available dish.
    'We oughtn't to have come here, mother,' said Paul.
    'Never mind,' she said. 'We won't come again.'
– D.H. Lawrence, Sons and Lovers

I

She had the first Renault Scenic in Perth. She was like that. She set trends. Other people watched her closely: where she shopped – which she did a lot – what she ate, who she slept with. A local style-heroine. The Scenic was a silver and grey four-wheel drive. The sort mothers would kill to be waiting in outside the posh private school at three in the afternoon. It looked to me like a stylish alpine climbing boot. It was drawn in towards the front giving a tightly laced look. And the matt black roof-racks were the suede trim around a very French ankle.

The car park, its ugliness apparently tolerated because of its functionality, was filling up fast on Friday evening. I was giddy from having taken the tight bends up seven floors. There it was, her definitive silver-grey accoutrement, parked like a Chanel handbag in the open lockers behind the desk in the art gallery. Now I was giddy with the anticipation of meeting her. A sprig of honeysuckle nestled loosely in my palm. It was not concealed in embarrassment; more like a little secret of ours. This anticipation of meeting was one of the delicious feelings between us. If she arrived first, as on this occasion, she would make a satisfactory space for us. She'd done this in the hotel rooms which we frequented when we first had sex. Now she was doing it again. Finding a suitable corner in the restaurant and studying the menu for when she would, like a mother, order for both of us. While she did that I moved deftly through the car park and along the street, crowded with Friday night shoppers and theatregoers.

We travelled in time, backwards and forwards, restlessly looking for a place our relationship might settle. Often to a time when we were young and free. The Japanese cafe where we had arranged to meet was perfect for this. It was new, it was foreign, and we could be in it together as if we too were new. But we were not young and not naive, we knew our love was out of step with the times. She was too practical for consulting literature on these matters; alone, I searched for previous personal anchorages which might help me to make more sense of what I was now participating in. Literature is like that: it can reach back, it can meet the present, and it can meet a time in the future previously beyond the grasp of experience. Re-consulting *Sons and Lovers* met me in the new place with new views on my old self.

I imagined a scene free of our current constraints where we were both young and where, instead of having to traverse the next twenty-five years of my painful experience, I might have learnt not some but all of what my early reading had to teach me. In this daydream I imagined we had grown up in the same town, on the same continent. I was at university, she in the last year of school. She was young and confident. She walked with her back straight and she stood out against the prevailing girls-boarding-school shuffle. She made her dark blue uniform look like a fashion statement. As I was lounging on the lawn in front of the library she came and stood in front of me, her shadow on the page I was reading. I was trying to look cool. A self-possessed, waiting-for-my-friends-but-fine-on-my-own look. The book was *Sons and Lovers*, the passage I was reading disturbing in a dark way unlike the pleasing disturbance Clara was about to be.

She broke away from her group of friends and walked almost defiantly across the lawn to me. My inclination was to look over my shoulder to see who she might be walking towards so purposefully but I didn't have time. I didn't once take my eyes off her. She smiled and in her two last paces said: 'I'm sorry, ooow I'm interrupting your reading, my friends and I are lost.'

The words tumbled out effortlessly. Stunned by her approach, I made no move from my slouching position on the grass so she knelt down. I was overwhelmed; she was much closer than most of my friends came to me. Trying to remain cool I heard my voice jag horribly in my throat.

'Ah, well you, see this is the library.' I gestured to the huge modernist building in front of us. God what a stupid thing to say, I thought, anyone could see that's the library. She seemed undeterred by my blundering.

'Ah yes it's a beautiful building isn't it?'

The library, a beautiful building? I hadn't thought of it that way before and made a mental note to look at it again sometime when this beautiful challenge was not in front of me.

'Well yes.' Blurted this time. Damn, I seemed to have no control over the volume of my voice which sounded fourteen again.

'We're going to a science quiz. We've no idea where it is, ooow oow I'm afraid we're such fools. And these uniforms are so sad. Sorry. The Main Science Lecture Thingy is the building we're going to.'

I was utterly charmed. Smitten in the first paragraph.

'Well I can show you where that is. I'd be happy to walk you there.' I was finally getting control of my voice and what it was saying. Even my legs were beginning to work now and I got to my feet, registering a blurry group of three more school girls huddling twenty metres away.

'Oh no! No we wouldn't want to take up your time.'

'No trouble at all, I've got days before my next lecture.'

She laughed. It was meant to be funny, that was good. Then again she surprised me.

'I'm Clara.'

'Andrew,' I bleated, my voice was gone again at her advance, even my legs didn't feel so good any more.

Even in my imagination, it took two more days and a lot of encouragement from my friend Alan – who said she might have friends he'd be interested in – for me to call her. I asked her to meet in town, Friday night at six. She said yes. I was jubilant, victorious and intrepid.

If it *had* happened then, I wouldn't have been old enough to know the meaning of this experience of our first meeting. But looking back, at forty, I'd have seen what it was: the main event, the challenge of the equal woman, the challenge to evade contempt.

II

The piece of *Sons and Lovers* that had disturbed me just before Clara boldly intruded on my reading was the scene in which Paul and his solicitous mother spend the afternoon in Nottingham together. It begins with the extravagance of lunch where Paul ineffectively resists his mother's indulgence of him. Later, shopping, Paul is caught between responding to his mother's joy and hiding away with her from the unwanted attention of the elegant shop-girl. They admire the paintings, the clothes, the fruit and finally the flowers:

'Now, just look at that fuchsia!' she exclaimed, pointing.

'H'm!' He made a curious, interested sound. 'You'd think every second as the flowers was going to fall off, they hang so big an' heavy.'

'And in such abundance!' she cried.

'And the way they drop downwards with their threads, and knots!'

'Yes!' she exclaimed. 'Lovely!'

'I wonder who will buy it!' he said.

'I wonder!' she answered. 'Not us.'

'It would die in our parlour.'

'Yes, beastly cold, sunless hole; it kills every bit of a plant you put in, and the kitchen chokes them to death.'

The home they return to is choking and cold, but mother and son have spent a perfect afternoon together, they arrive happy and glowing and tired.

It was a scene that at the time, at nineteen, I found strangely upsetting, though back then, I could not say why.

Though my earliest memory is of looking at flowers in the garden from my mother's hip, shopping was never happy with my mother. There had been no pleasure in it, and I had known so well the twist of pained guilt in the stomach that went with spending money rashly. I had felt the dark protectiveness towards my mother but mine was not borne of the experience of money being spent profligately on me. All I could remember was the cold and precise voice my mother used on the phone on Monday mornings when she ordered the groceries. I was embarrassed she sounded so haughty, so entitled to service. The boxes would be delivered later that afternoon by a black man who ran in from a van, his hands holding the boxes above the barking dog. I loved to unpack these boxes, though things were seldom as I wished. Why, I wondered, did my mother buy packets of mixed dried fruit when all the family didn't like apples and prunes? On rare trips to the grocery shop I had pointed out the packets of apricots or pears, but there was always the same austere formula. Food was a functional thing, to be organised and ticked off. One did not indulge oneself when eating or drinking. I didn't realise at the time the depths of this distortion, representing as it did the emotional poverty of the relationship itself.

Clothes were functional too. No choice; no forming of taste. New clothes appeared on my bed ready to wear. I remember shopping for school clothes only. McCullagh & Bothwell sounded like a quality shop to me and I liked the fact that the school prescribed items of clothing. I trusted the school's choice in these things more than I did my mother's.

How had my maternal grandmother managed to have such a different attitude to shopping? Granny would stop on the way to school and let me run into the Greek shop for sweets – Callard & Bowser liquorice toffees or Pascall fruit pastilles. Then there were the outings to town. Often we'd have been at the chores for no more than half an hour before she'd say indulgently to me: 'I think it's time for a cup of tea, let's pop up to Fatties.'

I knew very well that meant cream doughnuts for both of us. I loved her for that and never thought about the money or the indulgence, only the way it felt, as though something fitted me. 'As though something fitted me' would have expressed my feeling about *Sons and Lovers*, though the English department helped filter such sentiment and I knew better than to mention such Oedipal allusions in the psychology department. It would take so long for the fog of my youth to clear so that I could see some of the fullness of Lawrence.

III

I arrived at the restaurant out of breath with the pace of my walking and the anticipation of her. I would have to tell her my imagined prequel in front of the library; she did so like modernism. Shopping with her was pure cream-doughnut delight. Whether we were looking for new cooking utensils, second-hand furniture, or new clothes, the world seemed all new to both of us. Flirting with each other, we made friends with shop assistants; we bought lots of things for each other as well as for ourselves; it was hours before we flopped into a cafe. A cup of tea for her and iced mineral water for me. I learnt so much from her in these shopping expeditions. I learnt how to question the assistants, whereas before I'd always had to appear as if I knew what I wanted. She said, 'What's best for taking hot stuff out of a wok?' and, 'How do you think these earrings go with this colour?' and she asked me too. She walked determinedly around the clothes shop picking out all the things she thought would look nice on me and I tried them on and gave her little fashion parades in the passage of the change rooms. I practised her way of asking the young attendant what she thought of the clothes, though they smiled and agreed with everything *she* said. Sometimes I'd pull her to me in the change room and whisper in her ear and she would exclaim 'Oooh! You are such a naughty man!' I learnt her craft, her shopping craft. It reached far back to nurturance and to the glimpses I'd had at being loved out in the world by my grandmother. Because shopping had otherwise been such a depriving experience for me, I was learning to nurture myself and to develop my own style.

And when the shops were closing and we made our way back to the seventh story of the car park, I lay with my head in her lap as she sat in the driver's seat of the silver and grey fashion statement. We'd have to divide up the packages and drive home in different directions but we were as happy and fulfilled as teenage lovers after their first ever trip to the city together.

reading and writing

apartheid, *n. (S.Afr.). Racial segregation.*
[Afrikaans(apart, —hood)]
slum, *n.* **1.** *Overcrowded and squalid back street or court or alley or district in city.*
2.*v.i. Go about the —s to visit or examine conditions of inhabitants.*
township, *n. ... small town or village forming part of a large parish ...*

– The Concise Oxford Dictionary

I

'Mrs Joubert says you're having difficulties with your spelling.'

The way she said it made me think it may be a moral issue, something I needed to sort out with God. My mother had that knack. Sundays offered a kind of hopeful end to a week of personal flaws and failure.

'She says you've got a good imagination.'

A consolation prize. I don't think I answered but I know more or less what response I felt: Imagination? What is that? How does that help?

It didn't. They didn't give marks for imagination in spelling tests on Wednesdays. (Forty years later, I pause as *Wednesday* emerges onto the laptop screen: is that *d* really meant to be before that *n* or would it look better after it? Even now it's an aesthetic judgement.)

By the second year of school, illustrating Bible stories and cutting shapes out of strongly contrasting coloured paper no longer took up most of the day. All the letters had been practised. No problem there. Rows and rows of neat *t*s and *p*s. Coloured stars for good work and the tight little red initials identifying a perfectionistic but homely teacher. School was a joy, but now it was words. Words to be read and words to spell. Even with this added burden, I had a vague sense of optimism with two- and three-letter words:

He can bat the ball.
She has got the dog.
I can do it!

Then came the story book, and the realisation that none of the slim volumes, however elementary, told a story with two- and three-letter words alone. More was required.

Spelling tests began; they were out of ten. The teacher called out words in a clear and deliberate voice that shaped each syllable. To me the voice had a sort of mocking sheen: 'I'm really giving it away, saying it this clearly. Could anyone *not* know how to spell it?'

We wrote the words from the ruled-up margin, one on each line. I needed thinking time. The next word would be coming soon. The perfect letters I had practised squashed and fell over each other in my haste. Sometimes I would break off and go on to the next, my plucky breath shortening. Always when I returned, the tumbling start I'd made left no indication of the word required. Mostly, I didn't return; there was no time. The last perfect pronouncement dying away in the air, a silent look from the teacher would send the boys at the front of each row scurrying up the aisles to collect the books. I never sat in the front. I was never chosen and, anyway, it seemed unwise. I would sometimes get two right. The teacher, with child's printing, the graphic version of that voice, placed the correctly spelt word just across from mine. Every test was a kind of dull and predictable humiliation. I understood the little red *2* that sat on top of the line with the little red *10* below it long before I mastered the idea of fractions. In case I didn't realise my failure, the teacher often wrote a cramped comment:

Poor effort.
Write out for homework.
Learn them.

Sometimes her comments were quite unrelated to the spelling itself: *Untidy work.* Worst, the ones that used my name: *You must concentrate Andrew.* Or later, simply: *Andrew, really!* The inclusion of the name was supposed to demonstrate caring, a personal touch. Instead, I worried most about these comments and the ones with an exclamation mark. Often both these signals of sarcastic attack were present. My disability had not been recognised and so the comments felt like disingenuous invitations to join in where I felt constitutionally apart. The return of the exercise books meant failure, but I was relieved. It was over for another week.

Yet I had started to think about myself as someone who couldn't read or write. If you'd asked me, at the time, some question skilfully designed to elicit the child's sense of identity it would have been there, resting just below the surface.

The classroom in which I suffered this weekly torment was basic but it was hung around with bright pictures; light radiated in from the north through a bay window and in winter the four-inch copper piping that ran around the walls a few inches off the ground was good to put your feet on. We all wore warm blazers and at exactly ten-thirty there would be a knock at the door. The teacher would stop, go over and open it. There would be the same familiar face, indefinably bowed down and resigned. At a signal, the front-desk favourite would jump up and take the tray with fifteen little bottles of milk from the man. I don't remember the boy's name but the man was called Mr Kumalo. He was black and the *Mr* was a liberal affectation. It reflected neither status nor respect but the espoused values of a white, Christian, middle-class school in Johannesburg in the 1960s. The school motto was One and All, a vaguely Christian version of the catastrophically ironic apartheid South African motto: *Ex Unitate Vires* – From Unity, Strength.

The school itself sprawled around the focal point of the ivy-clad chapel. Three panels of stained-glass windows depicted the parable of the Good Samaritan – a hopeless gesture of compassion in our heartless political context. There were two wings of classrooms around lawn quadrangles. Further, up a flight of Palladian steps, two boarding houses and, between them, a large kitchen and dining room. Sports fields with a pavilion. And all this held, as in a nest, in a large containing-and-excluding forest. Three hundred and forty acres of privilege. Our school, a curious site of disadvantage.

There is always a greater context. Through the accommodating forest where we built tree houses was a highway busy with traffic and then a fence with litter blown up against it by the icy breezes. The highway sliced reality. On the far side, corrugated iron lean-tos were patched with cardboard and plastic that billowed and tore. Blankets were thin and hunger pushed out the bellies of six year olds. The dread there was a sickness called *kwashiorkor*; across the highway, spelling. It's difficult for a child to see outside the boundaries.

Years later, I'm as reliant on the spell-check function of my computer as I am on a mechanic to fix my car. It's not a joyous, victorious experience. Those spellings from fifty years ago where my pencil stabs and *her* perfect red-ink corrections stood side by side, still echo. In a strange replay of my early dismay I stare, sometimes for several seconds, as the word processor selects first my word and then, underneath it, the word it thinks I really meant to write. My eyes flick between them – I cannot tell them apart. Mostly this is a mechanical and dull process. Occasionally, unbidden and without warning, I feel the sudden pang of red initials scratched somewhere on the interior surface.

There are other problems with this wonder software invention. Write a word correctly spelt for another meaning and the computer doesn't spot the error. These double agents that go unnoticed will humiliate and unmask the six year old. *Principles, stares, councils, bares* and *whether* all slip through the e-net and into someone's entertainment. In a primitive memory of classroom shame, improperly spelt words are entertaining. The more improperly, the more entertaining. Rude and treacherous English.

Then, the most secret problem of all: I feel it as a confession. The spell check nominates the word I've typed but offers no word to replace it. That cryptic teacher's comments have become a blinking cursor: *You're so wrong, that I can't think of anything you could be confusing it with.*

This is the problem I had with dictionaries as a child.

'What's the point of having a dictionary unless you know more or less where to go looking in it?' I asked my incredulous mother. A dictionary needed a sympathetic intermediary.

Poor speller: 'N ... what? ... to look up naive.'

'N – A ...'

'N – A ... what? You might as well spell the whole word.'

The dictionary I bought when I went to university became one of my best loved books. Though in the early days, it was a tempestuous relationship, a troubling affair based on the intrigue of the unknown. Now weathered, as I am, it remains my constant companion when I write and a confident source of exploration when I read.

II

In the year I was eleven, boredom settled on our house in the suburbs on a Saturday like a relentless heat that builds through the afternoon. Only Sunday afternoon ennui was worse. I can easily relive the experience now. My mother and sister sleep. My brother is in his room. Something has to happen, such emptiness cannot be sustained. It may rain; a motor car might career out of control in the street in front of the house; five chickens might walk in through the back gate; the enormous pine tree in the garden over the street from us might explode in the first and most charged bolt of lightning before the oncoming storm. All these things did happen in that house in Dudley Road, but never in that house on a Saturday afternoon. No longer able to bear the suspense, I wandered up the passageway towards my brother's bedroom. My desultory index finger trailed along the stippled surface of the painted wall and leapt in a slow arc across two open doorways. I stood in the entrance to his room and said nothing. He was lying on his side, his head propped up on his elbow. He made the bed look comfortable. With his left hand he supported the left pages of a hardback book. He knew I was there, but his concentration didn't wander from the page. I watched as he finished the left page and tipped the book up to read the right page. Then, with his thumb and forefinger, he turned the page. He repeated the movement with a kind of slow rhythm. I watched him doing this for several minutes. He turned six or seven pages. I realised that there was a page-turning technology here. He was reading unconsciously. The issue was not eyes and page, but the story alone. We didn't speak.

I went back to my room. I went via the inviting glass doors of the bookcase in the hallway which smelt of wood polish and volumes from the fifties. I selected *Biggles in the Cruise of the Condor* and took it, like a great treasure, to my room. There, full of expectation, I lay on my side, propped my head up and opened the book. Boredom evaporated in that stamp-album smell. The foxed title page I could turn like my brother did. The writing on the next page started halfway down; this I'd also be able to do quickly. By the third sentence my thoughts drifted as I began to imagine the picture. I hadn't read a page yet and I was encountering the wild places of South America and the brave flying men. When I finally did turn the page, the turgid scene-setting that I encountered seemed dull and condescending in comparison to my imaginings. My foot was itchy. I was on the second page. I would have to let the book fall closed so that I could scratch. When I picked it up again it felt heavy in my hand and it opened at the title page. I was going to read this book, but lying down made me feel tired. Perhaps I should sit up at my desk in the corner of the room. I rose and walked across the room. Sovereign, the large biscuit-coloured dog, my favourite family member, was directly outside my window. He was lying in the sun. With a sad weight of dissatisfied longing I went out to join him.

III

These days, forty years later, I have learnt to read, but the process is still laborious and I have two main ways of going about it. Either I choose to read every word and punctuation of a poem, every word of a short story, every line of a novel, or I take a kind of sampling from journal articles, textbooks, newspapers, or prospective books. Unlike most serious readers, I read nothing I don't want to read. I'm like a person with a breathing problem, restricting themselves to oxygen or at least to clean air. This style of reading, I realise, has made literature densely important to me. At first it was a rich fabric I wrapped myself within; later it seemed to infuse me with my own identity, the backbone and ribs of my personality; and now it is a deeply necessary pleasure.

Let me show you one more scene of how hard I tried and how envious I was of others in pursuit of writing and reading.

I am nineteen. The big clock hands of the examination hall move toward time-up as I write hyperactively at my desk. I'm halfway through the fourth and last essay. It will be miraculous if I pass, and such sweet revenge on my school teachers. I refocus my mind on Conrad's characterisation in *Nostromo*. Now the beaked woman has got up from her chair at the front of the hall. For the last twenty minutes she has been sitting motionless except for her roving eyes. A crow perched in judgement. Now her movement is preliminary to her saying something as if she is clearing her throat with her body. She is gathering herself for her mighty pronouncement: the order for us to stop writing. I write two more explosive sentences. She looks at her watch and then back to the large clock at the front. Seeing her movement, students begin to move and murmur as the audience does between movements at a symphony concert. No words, just a readying to break out of the constraints of the last three hours. Two more sentences: I need ten more minutes to finish. It is then that I look over to the woman at the desk across the aisle. She is proofreading her work and underlining the titles of the books she has quoted. She looks cool. How can she look that good at the end of three hours?

'STOP WRITING!! Close your examination books and make sure that your student number is in the top right hand corner. Label your second book and place it in the cover of the first.'

Second book? Some people wrote two books! Jesus, this is bad! I look across the aisle again. Yep, Ms F.R. Leavis has got two books over there. Two books of proofread essays with the titles underlined. She sees me looking and smiles; my return smile is wan, the one people give the camera when they've been pulled out of the water by the rescue team after capsizing their yacht. I snap my single exam book closed with some irritation. One word – written twice on the last page of hurried script catches my attention: *Tolled*.

Shit, that's bells. I meant recounted – *told*.

They will laugh in the staff room or maybe just shake

their condescending heads.

In the same year, I joined SPARSEC. It's indicative that I can't remember what the acronym stood for, but judging from the activity, it was probably Student Provided Arithmetic Reading and Spelling Education Classes. We were second- and third-year students, mostly Arts. Though I didn't have time on my hands, others did. Each Wednesday we drove the fifteen kilometres out of the university town to a black slum the authorities euphemistically called a township. We were slumming, but not *slumming it* – yet another euphemism. Between two and six we conducted several classes each. Our students were mostly adults, some kids, learning to read simple sentences and to write business letters: *Dear Sir/Madam, re: Delivery Boy Job.*

It wasn't our business to incite them to change the job description to *courier*, though by now most of us were recognising real disadvantage when we saw it. Literature helped with this – to more clearly envisage the self, the other, and the context. The closer I came to language the more my vision opened up. At school our South African history book had no chapter five; we were told the government had taken it out. Sitting there with Sipu, perhaps ten years older than me, who always wore a tailored cream suit, or with Beauty, whose five children she wanted to help get along in life, I was learning to see outside the boundaries within which I had been raised.

intermezzo

authentic, *a. Reliable, trustworthy; of undisputed origin, genuine. f. Gk,* authentikos *one who does a thing himself.*
– The Concise Oxford Dictionary

Dear Reader,

I identify with being a reader more than a writer.

I remember my mother reading to me. Occasionally others read to me too: teachers to the class at school; perhaps my grandmother. But my mother's reading has a particular significance; it is that I don't remember any other major sense of nurturance from her. Writing is what my mother fed me. Other people's stories were the fountainhead. They were stories about attachments and emotions. Stories of love and deep grief. They were often about children. Sad stories like E. Nesbit's *The Railway Children* and another called *Circus Life*. An endless diet of library books which, unlike our regular food, was rich with choice and selection. The richness on which I fed in those first books was the richness of emotion; often it was children whose emotions were depicted: joy, loss, comfort, security, fear, wonder. I listened for these emotions in the stories I was read, and I felt them. Was this merely luck or did my mother sense her emotional deficiency in relation to my need, and do at least what she could?

I remember the van that would pull up in the street outside our semi-rural house. The driver, a young woman with short curly hair, glasses and flat shoes would open the single door towards the rear of the van and fold down the metal steps. My mother and I would enter the cramped, book-lined interior which, without windows, was often intolerably hot. All the books were covered with plastic and they had perplexing numbering on the spines.

That night we'd begin. It was like setting out on a journey. There would be strange places and adventurous action, but above all there would be new people. And the people would be engaged with one another in such a way as to produce deep emotional responses, each in the other and all in me. We went one chapter at a time until the book was completed and ready for exchange. It was only through the pleasure of selecting a new book that the pain of releasing one that had been read was assuaged. How could we give back this collection of people we'd had a relationship with these last ten days? The story may have ended but I had no sense that the characters had left. The idea that you would stop reading a book because you had got to the end seemed somehow strange and upsetting.

The obvious thing for a parent to say was: 'Stop

complaining, Andrew. We'll get a new one tomorrow.'

'But this is the one I want to read more of.'

'Well, we'll get it out again sometime.'

Was it Anthony Trollope who said that no one gets in closer to the reader than the novelist, not even his mother?

At seven I had a deep understanding that reading a book was a relationship. Is it possible that the shortcomings in my relationship with my mother enhanced this feeling for me? It was certainly true that my lack of facility for reading for myself inspired the regular reading my mother undertook with me. This triangular relating – the book, my mother and I – set up in me an expectation that all books offer a relationship. Later, when I read alone, I seldom sustained reading a book without this sense of a relationship. I was aware that other people were reading quickly and superficially, but I was stuck with a ponderous and intense way of reading which left no time for any frivolous reading outside a close relationship. I've never had a literary one-night stand, never even a gratuitous weekend away with a book.

Years later, when studying psychology, I came across attachment theory: the attempt by psychologists to understand the bonds of relatedness which develop first in infancy and later which become characteristic of many of the individual's relationships. Attachment theorists focus on the most influential of relationships and their disturbance, principally that between mother and child. Reading literature in the area, I came to recognise how my attachments had been disrupted. And later, how I became a reader and a psychotherapist partly in response to these disruptions. I came to realise too that my attachments had been constituted in some unusual places but that this was not at all uncommon amongst those people who came to see me for psychotherapy. I became particularly interested in how people other than parents can fulfil early attachment needs and how these *others* may include non-human and inanimate objects. Where my family members may have felt to me insufficient or lacking in relatedness, I found myself experiencing significant connection with places, like my school or my house; with music and pictures; with animals, especially my dog; with people who would not have seemed to others, because of the relatively little time I spent with them, to have been significant attachment figures. One very special category of these alternative attachments for me was the books I read and those that peopled them.

These alternative childhood attachments were not encouraged in me. My mother's primary attachment was to God and the church, a lifelong devotion, which probably emerged from *her* disrupted attachments and *her* unresolved grief. This devotion limited and bent the early pattern of my relationship with her. It also led her to disallow my emerging attachments to others. In particular, my relationships with characters from stories, pictures, my dog, the bird in the cage, were somehow sacrilegious, immoral, and I learnt to keep them to myself. Yet the books which she shared with me in my childhood and with which I did something much more than she would ever have imagined, set me on a lifelong rehabilitation.

In Anne Michaels' novel *Fugitive Pieces*, Jakob is a boy recovering from unspeakable horror and Athos, his new parent figure, assists in his rehabilitation by telling him stories and by reading to him from an old and encyclopaedic library containing books of poetry, history, botany, insects, animal navigation, scroll painting, Greek independence, palaeontology.

Athos's stories gradually veered me from my past. Night after night, his vivid hallucinogen dripped into my imagination, diluting memory.

Mine was a simpler, less global, debilitation. What I needed were principles of relationship and the tangled emotions which are encoded in them. I needed my imagination to be validated and complemented. I needed storybooks, novels, to veer me from my past and towards emotional understanding.

All my adult life I have been reading two or three books at any one time. I am one of those readers who has a comforting stash of five to ten books on my bedside table. And when I complete a book, which I don't do very often – starting as I do many more than I complete – they stay a while in a prominent place around the house. I cannot easily put them away. Even when I do consign them to the populated anonymity of the bookshelves, they seem to glow with a kind of attachment which, now latent, can be initiated again merely by taking them in my hands and reading a few lines from anywhere in the book.

With this kind of attitude to reading and to books, dear Reader, how should I see my relationship to you? What is the responsibility of the reader? What is the responsibility of the writer? How should we think about this relationship?

As an author roused into writing by reading – was there ever any other type? – this letter comes to you from a fellow reader. It must be true for all writers that they are more fundamentally readers. Isn't writing just another form of reading and reading just another form of writing? But I know that few authors write as if this were true. They don't refer much to the relationship between themselves and the reader, well not as much as they used to do, and when they do it often seems patronising – you the reader, a regrettable necessity in my higher calling as author. Is this my old vulnerability as a reader surfacing again, or do you feel this too? Recent authors, with some notable exceptions, seem somehow disconnected from the reader and the activity of reading. They separate the two activities. Shakespeare by contrast appears to esteem his readers, his theatregoers, often seeming grateful to them, to us, without mocking or sarcasm. The prologues, for example to *King Henry VIII*, not only prepare the audience but start the relationship which is to ensue – even broaches the money involved in the transaction. And at the end of *A Midsummer Night's Dream* how sublime is the parting between author and reader:

> Puck: *If we shadows have offended,*
> *Think but this – and all is mended –*
> *That you have but slumber'd here*
> *While these visions did appear.*

Most *Dear Reader* notes appear at the outset of a book; I address you now because I want to relate to you as a fellow reader as much as a writer. This is a journey from reading to writing. It's about here that I first feel confident enough in my role as writer to address you, the reader. All the relatively recent ideas about the reader being involved in the book they are reading – that the reader somehow brings the literature alive because they are bringing their imagination to the text they are reading – seems to me to have been self-evident since writing and reading began. Certainly it was clear to me when I began to read. Let me use, for a moment, the metaphor of the psychotherapist, my day job. I can't do psychotherapy without someone in my office to do it with. But when I call what I do *a special sort of conversation,* other psychologists can sometimes get offended. They would say that such a specialised occupation cannot be defined as just a conversation. Whereas I think that conversation is such a special sort of thing that it should be taken as a compliment by the profession. But, while I can't do psychotherapy without a person in my room, there are nevertheless psychotherapists who, even when they do have a person in their room, don't have a conversation with them. They may listen, and they may say what their response is to what they have heard, but they do not make a new relationship; they do not create something in the space between the client and themselves. Just so, I have read books where no conversation was going on between me and the author, no space between the written lines for me to become more the person I am. This is the responsibility of the author. They are the context-setters into whose terrain the reader invites themselves, looking for something.

I was taught that visitors when they leave should say, 'Thank you for having me.' To which the host should say, 'You're welcome' or, 'Thank you for coming.' I think of you, the reader, as being someone who has invited themselves into my writer's territory, but in publishing a book I have made an invitation to the reader. Like a cyber-dating agency I have placed my profile on the net. But how unusual that I should then cease to have any say about who picks me up. I do, however, have a say about what people will make of the book. A skilfully written book will leave room both for the reader and for the writer. Engaging you in this way will leave you with work to do and the chance of enjoyment, stimulation, consolation, identity. It will be a conversation. But, dear Reader, this is not a modern concept. Laurence Sterne's *Tristram Shandy*, written in the 1760s and arguably one of the first novels in the English language, contains many exchanges, some more lucid that others, between author and reader. Sterne's intentions in this respect couldn't be clearer: *Writing when properly managed (as you may be sure I think mine is) is but a different name for conversation ...*

What about this territory of mine into which you are invited? Isn't it strange how discrete the novel seems to need to be? To stand entirely on its own. To live up to its name – all new. I think it's an ego thing for the author which doesn't fool the reader. It's like the little fences that run all the way round the rows of houses between two streets in the suburb in which I live. I sometimes wonder what would happen if our block – about forty houses – decided to put a fence round the street-side only. We'd have this enormous five-acre garden and the kids and the dogs would have more space to move. Novels have fences round them. The fences cut the story off from other novels and from other sorts of writing that would not be classed as a novel.

This in answer to a query on the phone from my ageing mother: 'Yes Mum, I'm writing literature, but not exactly a novel. That's because I don't want to fence it in too much. Don't get me wrong, it's not just a pile of undisciplined ravings.'

But Mother doesn't listen; she's quickly on to a retort: 'Ah, but son, writing which isn't fenced in doesn't do very well in the end.'

I think she means that lack of fencing leads to a breakdown in the coherence of things. I refer to the metaphor again. I think this idea of no dividing fences around property has been tried. I've stayed in something similar in Stockholm and London. I assume it's only worked where some functional rules about how things work without fences have first been established.

Architects say there are no new buildings; I heard Frank Gehry say that this is the comforting thought with which he begins a new project – he says it's his safety-net, his parachute. At least he isn't trying for anything new! And many authors would say that they start from a similar position of there being no new stories. But if that is true, why is it that so few writers say anything about the books that have influenced them? You can say that my writing territory is specifically the books that have influenced me, but novelists may put that into a code of their own, a disguise. Anne Michaels, who I mention elsewhere, doesn't elaborate on the poems that were so specifically helpful to Jakob in his recovery. It is unusual for characters in the novel to read as much, or with as much benefit as one would imagine them to – though my mind goes quickly to several exceptions: *Northanger Abbey*, *Orlando*, *David Copperfield* and, more recently, Martin Amis's *The Pregnant Widow*. My point, dear Reader, is that writing is the end product of reading, and that less distinction between the writer and the reader may be desirable.

My invitation to you is substantial. It is about authenticity. Perhaps I always read with an eye on the writer's authenticity, but now I do so increasingly. Authentic and author share the same genetic forebear – the Greek *authentikos* means 'one who does a thing himself'.

So, you should expect authenticity from me. The invitation is into the heart of my experience when I tell you about the reading. This is my responsibility, both to myself and to my reader, and it leaves you with an increased responsibility yourself. Not to me, so much as to yourself. If this is, as I suggest, a relationship, a conversation, then you owe it to yourself and not just to me to allow this material to work on you. Either that, or stop reading and give the book away.

I have tried to leave space between the words and the lines for you. But I have also tried to keep irony out of my writing, at least that most sarcastic form of it, which excludes rather than includes. Which hides rather than reveals the author's thoughts and feelings. That brand of irony corrodes authenticity. The other irony which delights in the power of words and in the perverseness of things, the one to which we are all equally victim, suits me better. But, in avoiding the disguise of irony and trying to stay with an intellectually less defensive mode, I have nevertheless not wanted to be sentimental or self-indulgent in my prose. Someone once said that sentimentality is unpaid-for emotion. Mine is paid for.

And, unlike irony, which seeks to confer an inner meaning for a privileged audience, I have sought to make metaphor the heart of my writing. It is metaphor which connects us all and metaphor which allows us the space to bring ourselves to the story. It is from this coherent figurative backdrop that we find light being cast upon our individual experience. This is very close to the work of psychotherapy. A triangle between the reader, this book and me.

Rest assured too that I have already been compensated for the value of the words I have written. There is a relative worth in psychotherapy and a particular sort of reading, and I have found many similarities between them. Writing, where I have taken up a place in the other chair in the conversation, has an equal or greater worth for me than reading or psychotherapy.

So I leave you to the rest of my book. Like a parent I did not have, like a good psychotherapist, like the writers whose books have veered me from my past towards myself, I return to the background. And in that background, knowing a little of how I think and respond to things emotionally, you may feel me adopt a listening, reading position, pausing for your response between my words without which there would be no conversation, no literature.

Yours,
Fellow Reader

ignoring icarus

The youth in vain his melting pinions shakes,
His feathers gone, no longer air he takes:
Oh! Father, father, as he strove to cry,
Down to the sea he tumbled from on high
– Ovid, 'The Fall of Icarus'

I

There have always been stories, but in families – well, in my family – you can't always trust the veracity of those stories. They depend on who's telling them much more than on what actually happened. With literature, the contract is so much simpler: the author speaks and the reader interprets. Take the simple question of the big, brindled dog jumping up on my father in one of the sixteen millimetre films from my childhood. All these years later my mother has an elaborate story about how he came to live with us.

My parents were buying furniture from a house sale in

the neighbourhood. The owner, an old woman now on her own, was going into a retirement village.

'What will you do with the Great Dane?' my mother asked. The woman admitted, her face suddenly red and congested with tears, that she'd been unable to bring herself to do anything about alternative accommodation for her companion. He certainly couldn't go with her. So my parents acquired Sovereign, who became my companion and who gave me, at age two and ever since, a sense about dogs and their capacity for affection and devotion.

My father has different stories to tell about Sovereign and, quite unsolicited, said at one point: '... and you see, we'd got him from the RSPCA, I think.' At least he'd added that note of uncertainty.

Omniscient I was not, but *to look* was my survival. In the early family films which my father compulsively made, the pre-schooler is watching closely, never saying much. He seems perplexed. Sometimes he smiles in a shy but engaging way; sometimes he frowns. He seems uncertain. He seems in danger, and children who are in danger are vigilant. But the danger here is not dramatic. There are no stories of being smacked severely or of being traumatised in a traffic accident. Certainly none about going hungry or sleeping out in the cold, though two kilometres away in the black township children died at night. No, this danger was below the surface, a dark current beneath the carefully produced face of the family. It was about parents careless of a child's needs, a subtle absence, not something perpetrated by horrible people.

There are things I do remember from about then. The films project me back into my interior life to which I had often gone as a child, disconsolately wandering away from those around me.

I remember fabrics. The Sanderson Linen that covered the chairs in the lounge. Big, bold, rose prints. Those roses were so real to me that I thought I could smell their powdery pink perfume as I lay across them, always defying the concept of chair with my boy's body, agile and restless, legs over the arms and head near the carpet ... the colour now washed out from my memory, but the texture that I marvelled at still there. How, from up in the chair, it looked flat and smooth but then with my nose and mouth pressed against it, a forest would appear millimetres away from my eyes. A forest in which things could happen. Horses could appear; farmers, birds, and below them the earth; the criss-crossed brown backing of the carpet. The smell fitted too; it was earthy and dusty and too strong to keep inhaling. What did anyone make of the boy suspended in headlong dive, his face in the carpet? Was anyone looking?

The curtains in my bedroom also had a repeated pattern. I was in the thrall of these repeating things. They were less representative than the roses on the lounge furniture and I liked them more. They seemed to me repeated scenes, endlessly unfolding through grasses, past gates and fences, under willow trees, across water. The things of the world were there; not fully, just gestures and suggestions, leaving me to invent. I constantly checked to see if the end of the next duplicated pattern would put a different light on my construction, and sometimes it would because of the hanging folds of the curtains.

When the curtains moved was the best: then I could not only see all the images, I could hear a kind of echoing, calling, singing voice. The voice in my curtains was high-pitched, very melodic and so sympathetic it made me want to cry with the fullness of feeling it produced. When I heard Sarah Brightman's voice, as an adult thirty-five years later, I thought it was the closest thing to what I'd heard in my bedroom all those years before. Sentimental? No. Not now that I realise that my curtains, like my dog, could 'do' the sympathy I needed for the real emotions of childhood.

I do remember my mother's look of mild alarm when I told her one morning that I had seen a mother and a child in my curtains, and that the mother was tenderly cleaning the child's ears. She was puzzled and unable to respond.

So it is with bigger systems where things are going wrong: societies, countries. Watching turns to ignoring. Needs dip below the horizon and in their place appear conventions which seem, to those caught up in it, to be a sort of kindness. Take the English-speaking white people. They were kind to their servants. 'Kindness' meant the black woman could stay in the *kia*, the room out the back of the house, while her children went without medicine and warmth, looked after by another in the township. 'Kindness' meant she could have the rest of the day off on Sundays after the family ritual of the lunchtime roast. People were caught in the mesmerising appearances of normality when, all about them, suffering was ignored. I call it carelessness because it seems now to have been such a passive act to collude with the way things were.

Years later I got my best marks for an essay on the W.H. Auden poem, 'Musée des Beaux Arts':

> *About suffering they were never wrong,*
> *The Old Masters; how well, they understood*
> *Its human position; how it takes place*
> *While someone else is eating or opening a window or just*
> *walking dully along;*

The tragedy of Icarus is unfolding. He is falling to his death in the Aegean, while all around life goes on careless of his fate. I was a young man, passionate, yet strangely blind to what I wrote about:

> *The poet's message is simple and it is stated simply. The isolation of human suffering results as much from what the sufferer feels as from what the rest of the world fails to feel. The world should take greater concern in the predicament of the individual.*

My reverie connects here once more to the memories which flicker on, as my father's films used to on the white screen pulled from its metal casing in the lounge room of my family home. The crawling boy in blue dungarees is at his mother's side. He levers himself to stand next to her legs as she sits on a hay bale in the country. His intention is clearly to sit next to her on the roughly trussed up grass. He slaps lightly on her leg with his diminutive hand and looks up to study for a moment her face. The camera has studied her face. It is passive, composed, free of emotion. The eyes are looking away, into the distance towards the looming mountains. The boy hesitates a moment but, seeing that his motion has not gained his mother's attention, he continues, apparently unconcerned, to lever his young body up onto the seat alongside his mother. The moment is barely there before it is gone. The tone of the clacking projector changes to a flapping sound and the harsh unfiltered light comes up on the screen. The spool of film is at an end. Time to put on the lights.

At nineteen, Auden's poem helped me reach towards an initial understanding of where things stood with careless systems. In my essay I may have been fumbling towards an understanding of a social system whose personality had been disordered by apartheid, but I was then entirely unaware of the resonance with the carelessness in my own life. No one asked me for my personal associations to the last verse of the poem:

> *In Breughel's Icarus, for instance: how everything turns away*
> *Quite leisurely from the disaster; the ploughman may*
> *Have heard the splash, the forsaken cry,*
> *But for him it was not an important failure; the sun shone*
> *As it had to on the white legs disappearing into the green*
> *Water; and the expensive delicate ship that must have seen*
> *Something amazing, a boy falling out of the sky,*
> *Had somewhere to get to and sailed calmly on.*

If someone *had* asked me my personal associations, they would have been more about a careless father than a careless audience. If I had played one particular film from about the time of my sixth birthday I would have seen enough to jolt the trauma from its resting place in my memory.

My father had directed me to a slippery rock at the top of a small waterfall in the scenic Drakensberg for a holiday photograph. I remember my older brother, sensible of the danger, refusing to go. I presume the picture was never taken. If it had been, it would have shown a small boy in a headlong dive: white legs, forsaken cry; a boy falling out of the sky. Instead the still camera was packed away and the sixteen millimetre brought out to film the more interesting story of the events after the fall. A lot of blood and a few tears washed in the ice-cold berg stream. A makeshift bandage from my mother's scarf, tied at the top of my head to get the bleeding of the chin to stop. Sips of water from cupped hands. A brave smile to the whirring camera: what else could I do? There is a sequence too of the homeward journey, on horseback, which must have been painfully bumpy.

The fact that he recorded the results of his carelessness are suggestive of the disturbance in my father's psyche: his self-centredness; his inability to empathise.

I read Auden's poem when I was nineteen as one experiences an important dream at the moment of waking. Something deeply resonant washes through your emerging consciousness. There has been a palpable realignment of the repeating patterns deep in the recesses of one's mind. One feels grateful for such dreams but one cannot properly account for the sensation. Later, one can find meaning from studying the dream but the extent of its significance often remains imminent. A poem, like the patterned fabric on curtains and chairs, can create personal images which rouse in one comfort and distraction but which can also take many years to be seen in their full significance.

II

In his eighty-second year of life my father was doing his exercises one Sunday morning when, without warning, he fell backwards, hitting the side of his head on a linen cist on his way to the carpeted floor. His fear would have been immense as his wife ran in from downstairs having heard the heavy thud. He struggled to his knees, pushing her hand away with irritation. One leg moved half his body to standing and then he collapsed again.

I flew the six thousand kilometres from Perth to Auckland that night and, at dawn, was ushered to his bedside where he lay on his back. I could tell he was pleased to see me though his 'Hello sonny' had a desperate resignation indicative of his situation. I sat with him and told him of the holidays we'd had together, the fish we'd caught and the ships we'd sailed on. It was like a meditation, he held my hand and drifted in and out of sleep. I told him I thought he was very ill and tears of assent ran from his eyes.

After years of having to be careful for myself in relation to my father, the thing that surprised me most was how deep my sorrow was for him lying on his death bed. I could not have predicted the intensity of my sympathy for this dying man. It allowed me to love him for the first time as I love, without protective reserve, fully, openly and with a deep empathy that had always been foreign to him.

Later I buried him in a small graveyard on the side of a hill overlooking the beautiful Bay of Islands. It was a warm and sunny summer afternoon. And the cruise liner that was anchored in the bay did in fact have somewhere to get to, and sailed calmly on before the burial service was complete.

did you read doctor zhivago?

For poetry makes nothing happen: it survives
In the valley of its making where executives
Would never want to tamper, flows on south
From ranches of isolation and the busy griefs,
Raw towns that we believe and die in; it survives,
A way of happening, a mouth.
       – W.H. Auden, 'In Memory of W.B. Yeats'

I

Dr Geering was a Jungian analyst. I took my first dream to her like a precious offering: a water colour, a poem, a sonata. It had been glowing in my mind for two weeks since I'd made the appointment. I had scribbled detailed notes when I'd woken breathless with the after-image of my small white car careering out of control down the slope outside the university psychology department where I was an honours student. It was the start of the year following my special essay on D.H. Lawrence. I was privately disoriented by life, bewildered by relationships, and periodically depressed.

I noticed that a fellow student didn't treat his first session of psychoanalysis with the seriousness that I did. He told me he'd invented a dream, because he couldn't remember one which didn't incriminate him in some way or another. He said Dr Geering told him that he had this little thing in his psyche called a *shadow* and that once he'd dealt with that, he could get on with being a psychologist without fear of foisting his own problems on other people.

God! That was nothing like my experience. I knew that my dream was somehow going to be very significant. I told it in great detail and felt listened to with the same meticulousness. We discussed every image in the story and then she told me what it meant. I had never experienced anything like this kind of revelation. It was miraculous. I would have taken another appointment the next day if one had been available. She said I could have Tuesdays at five in the afternoon. It sounded like a regular date. There was nothing about three-session cures. She said I could call her Gloria and that I should keep a record of my dreams. Her name was like the session itself.

I'd also not missed the gloriousness of the Catholic mission compound where this analysis of my psyche was going to happen. The red brick buildings – hospital, monastery and staff houses – were spread out around the architectural centrepiece, a Byzantine-style chapel. Later I would go and sit in the church after some sessions and float in its cool, sweet-smelling spiritual air surrounded by coloured lights playing through indistinct pictures of the life of Jesus. My mother, after all, had scolded me as a child when I'd made the grossly inappropriate suggestion that I'd prefer to go to the Catholic church instead of our usual Methodist one. Gloria became my indulgent mother and this church, her aesthetic and spiritual arms.

It was as if, in psychoanalysis, I'd discovered a bulwark against bewilderment and an outlet for my imaginative creativity, my dreams. I was going to Gloria for instruction in how the psychological world really worked and how my personality could be explained. There was little conversation as I recall. I would talk and she'd say what it meant and what I should do about it. It was perfect for me, desperate as I was for wisdom and meaning. If I hadn't left the country, I may have stayed in Gloria's psychological arms for a very long time. With this kind of direct help I continued to need instruction; I was not really learning very quickly how to instruct myself. Perhaps what she offered was exactly what the child in me needed, a kind of re-parenting. But, although she might have thought my personality immature, I was not a child, and the problem with this arrangement was that feeling looked-after left me with little responsibility to look after the child myself.

For my part I encouraged this psychoanalytic parenting with Gloria. The novels I had been reading assisted me in the development of my emerging identity, but they did not offer what Gloria did. Literature seemed somehow less ambiguous in its demands on my development. Gloria, by contrast, appeared eager to continue her role as long as I offered her the child in me. Somewhere within the first three sessions, for example, I gave an account of my mother in which I included an incident when I was eight. My father and siblings were somehow absent that night and she had come into my room to tuck me in and say goodnight. I couldn't remember the words exactly but she had said that she was sick, that her heart was not beating right and that she was frightened that she may die in the night. Saying goodnight had felt like it might be saying goodbye. Perhaps my lifelong problem with sleeping started that night? Gloria sympathised.

I think I also told Gloria about an incident at the Rand Easter Show. This resources- and industrial-power display of a mining-rich Johannesburg in the late fifties was that city's answer to the gentler agricultural shows of smaller towns. I imagined myself to have been about six. We went at night to see the exhibits contained in large national pavilions before taking up our seats in the arena for displays of horse jumping, police on motorbikes, a flying man, and lastly, marching bands and fireworks. I had been excited for days in anticipation. There were people everywhere. Kids with toffee apples or candy-floss. The smell of animals and popcorn. Lights and banners and canvas and sawdust on the ground. It was like I'd stepped inside one of those fantastic drawings in which a million things are happening. When we had been there about ten minutes my mother crouched down in front of me and holding both my hands in a gesture of seriousness said: 'Stay close to us tonight, we don't want you getting lost.' That would have been all I needed to hear, but she went on, burdening my imagination to breaking point. 'If you do get lost ...' she turned my head with her hand, 'go to that building there. It's called the Tower of Light. There will be someone there who will put a message out on the loudspeaker for us to come and get you.'

It was indeed a tower of light – a tall square building perhaps five storeys high with a runnelled surface up which lights projected making it appear luminous in the night. There was one bright light in the shape of a flame at the top. I spent a good deal of that night checking that I could still see the Tower of Light and staying close by my family.

For years I ruminated on lost children. Gloria seemed like the perfect person to talk to about that subject.

My analysis lasted nearly four years. It was cut short, at least it felt unfinished, by my decision to get married and move to Australia. It seemed to me that there was no future for my profession as a psychotherapist in South Africa. It seemed an all-too-personal brand of activism for the times. So, one very cold June afternoon, my partner Susan and I were married in the lovely garden of her parents' house in the aptly named district of Winterskloof. Gloria is there in some of the photographs with one of her daughters. She wears the same all-knowing look which I had seen so often in our sessions. A kind of sad composure. Was it the residue of a life or was it the more immediate effect of her current observations, saying goodbye to her psychological son? Within a month I was courageously trying to find my way around a new city, a new country. I had more urgent discoveries to tax me, more obvious bewilderments to settle.

II

Twenty years later and surprisingly soon after our first meeting, my second psychotherapist said a little more definitely than was her usual style: 'There's a part of a mother that is a watcher.'

Of course that was true. Yet we both knew it to be true in different ways. She felt it to be a kind of biological force, an instinct. Images of this ran through my head. Nature was full of them: an ostrich hen shepherding five or six chicks in her giant shadow, craning her neck, scanning for danger; a prairie dog bitch; a she-elephant; ducklings marshalled in the eddying shallows alongside turbulent water. It was a stream of caring and protecting images. An insufficiency in a mother's watching had led me into this job of being a psychotherapist myself, watching others, a kind of mothering job.

The theme had returned, but the distance on *my analysis*, as I had taken to calling my time with Gloria, demanded a different treatment of the subject. I needed less nurturing education, less the emotional guiding hand, than I did an acknowledgement of the past so that I could negotiate the present north-west passage of my life.

'You've been watching your child for a long time.'

She made the statement with hardly enough volume to reach my ears yet it entered me with complete clarity. Pianoforte I thought. This is surely the role of the psychotherapist. The soft and the loud; the caress and the jab. But did she mean I should stop watching? Does a mother? The mother does stop, of course, but very slowly and just as much as she can be nearly certain her child is watching himself. *Nearly* certain because life, in order to progress, is always a risk.

'Did you read *Doctor Zhivago*, or perhaps see the film?' I enquired. She smiled, yes, but her smile was less in recognition as it was for the way I kept her so entertained. With Gloria I had only my dreams, I don't recall being allowed to introduce anything as secondary as Heathcliff and Cathy, Ahab or Heyst. Gloria may have seen them as defences against more urgent requirements. But here, at a later time in my life, I was free to rifle through my accumulated personal store of images, poems, novels, films, music. These things that could explain me, and the metaphors made for the moment, had already become a feature of our conversation. She seemed to restrain herself deliberately when I proffered them as if to enjoy their colour might make her vulnerable. But in the darkest moments I had nothing left over for her, I would stop choosing my words and cry as if I was being sick from my chest. Sometimes a great sobbing sigh would shudder through me and it felt like I was expiring. So it was here, merely asking her the question about the film had brought great gobs of grief to the surface. She waited quietly, almost tenderly, mother-like, watching.

'Well in *Doctor Zhivago*,' I drew myself together to continue speaking, 'one part of the tragedy is about people being lost because someone stops watching. A little girl feels her mother's hand let go of hers in the crowd, and she is lost forever. When you're in a revolution it's no time to stop watching the kid, and I'm in a revolution right now.'

In any case, I thought, what would happen if the injured child inside me continued to grow up, looking after itself, and reached maturity? Would it mean the end of my work as a psychotherapist? Perhaps the end of my drive to communicate, to relate? Would it be positive change or would the child be lost forever?

Then into my head, unbidden, an image of the little white angle figurine at the head of the grave, in the cemetery, at the end of the street where now I walk my dogs. How could something so anonymous be so full of personal meaning?

Angie, our beloved little one.
Gone so soon, aged two
Gentle be thy rest
And peaceful thy sleeping
God's way is best

I'd survived past age two in spite of frequent breathing problems. Past eight when my mother said she would die in the night. Past fourteen when my family split open. Past leaving home. Past migration. Past leaving the woman who had continued shepherding me when Gloria no longer did. It was not one more developmental stage to be mastered but all of them in a new way. Isn't this always the case? Why do we think things are got over, come to terms with, integrated, cured? I can see myself putting aside forever a self-help book – *Depression: Eight Steps to Happiness*, if ever I picked it up in the first place.

I'll never finish with *Doctor Zhivago*.

Yet Pasternak is an interesting case in point. David Lean

and the screenplay writer Robert Bolt who made the film from the novel must have got a much wider reading than Pasternak. I first saw the film as an early teenager. (Taking me to the movies was an ironic and desperately failed attempt by my mother and a neighbour to take my mind off the terrifying events unfolding in my family.) Implicitly recognising the literary symbols, the beauty of the writing in the film's beauty, I made several attempts to read the book which I borrowed from the public library. Yet I failed to unlock in the literature what had been unlocked from it by the film. The dense writing seemed overburdening to my slow and halting reading. Later, Pasternak's letters and poems helped me a little in my search for the original meaning. But I remain convinced that I have the novel itself as part of my reading and as part of my psychological development because of the film. I think Pasternak and I have a relationship thanks to David Lean. I feel grateful to both men. Together they instructed me in the nature of loss, love, betrayal, good deeds in bad situations and the sustaining impossibility of well-imagined outcomes. Literature contains, like written music, inspiration which will carry over to the reader. It allows, in fact sets up, the possibility that in any form, something of the essence will be there. As I write this, music fills the room like sunlight and I fully believe that Sir Georg Solti is the supreme master at delivering to my ears *A Hero's Life* by Richard Strauss. Yet, I realise that Strauss and Solti have formed a particular relationship and that on this afternoon I am the lowly yet necessary beneficiary of their extraordinarily rich legacy.

III

There was a man I once worked with who was ten years younger than me; in him I saw myself ten years before but without the experience of my psychoanalysis or my later psychotherapy. Such figures afford one a backward glance in the same way as one's parents do a forward one. Any such versions of the self are worth studying. Though he was not my patient, I wrote a clinical note about him to try to capture the familiar story:

Simon is a thirty year old psychiatrist. A young man going places. He has been asked to set up a new outpatient unit and he's thriving on the challenge. Yet the boy in him keeps attracting attention. Women particularly are intrigued by him, his energy attracts them, they want to look after him. These are women without children but with the instinct to be mothers. They see the boy in him and he responds. As an example, take a tantrum he has one morning when someone questions whether the good ideas he has just proposed are entirely his own. The challenge comes from a woman and a man on the team who probably see the boy in Simon as their childhood rival. They are sick of the smart little boy who always got the attention for being clever. They criticise him and he has no resilience, he cannot maintain his composure. He storms off to his office and, with his mind racing, tries to get on with his work. But there is a knock at his door and a young woman from the team walks in with a calming smile and a reassuring hand on his shoulder.

'Am I that useless?' he pouts. 'Am I that bad at handling people?'

'You're marvellous darling,' she whispers.

Her response is opportunistic and presumptuous of her position, she's never called him darling before, she's his junior in the organisation. For his part, the married man and father of two is completely overwhelmed by this reassurance. He will do anything for this woman. The boy in him will do anything for her. It is a narcissism which has made him so vulnerable.

The boy in him also comes to the attention of the team leader; he is magnanimous to Simon and sees the rough edges and they remind him of himself at that age. He does not counsel him about the need to look after the child in himself, he just smiles indulgently when he sees it in evidence and says, 'It's complicated, isn't it?'

But is he doing him a favour? Is he just waiting for him to fall? He'll be there to help him to his feet. But would he do better to take him aside and say: 'Simon, you have a responsibility here to yourself. The responsibility to truly look after yourself and stop putting little bits and pieces of yourself onto everyone around you.'

Yet this older man doesn't do this and the reason, if you asked him, is that the young man would reject his advice. Worse, he may feel criticised by his friend and mentor and become suspicious and inaccessible.

What about psychoanalysis? May that help?

Now, I imagine myself in conversation with Dr Geering. She is explaining herself, her treatment, perhaps to my later psychotherapist, perhaps to me.

'Doctor Geering, can you remember this as clearly as your young patient seems to be able to? What did you see as his struggles? What was your plan? What did you think he had to learn?'

Doctor Geering is seventy-three years old. I imagine she is, even now, strikingly attractive. Her hair is grey and thick and she still wears it long like a woman of much younger years. Her presence has a calmness about it, a deep spiritual steadiness. You feel as if you are encountering rather than meeting her. While her presence is so full, there is yet something opaque about her. Her eyes, her most remarkable feature, are very dark, and it is hard to distinguish the pupil from the iris. They are hung over by eyelids that are heavy. The overall impression from her gaze is of a person of great wisdom who is greatly tired. You might even ask, as you look at her, whether she is weary with life, depressed, waiting to die. Waiting for her reward for a life spent in the service of others.

'Well first let me say I make no apologies for my Jungian model and the methods of analysis that it proposes. I myself was analysed in Zurich and the method is perpetuated in this way. In fact I thought this particular young man was likely to make a very good analyst himself. When he came to me he was barely standing on his psychological legs. There was a lot I had to do for him. I found also that he was so receptive to my ideas and to my help that I spent more time with him than I might have originally planned.

'It might help to use a metaphor to explain the dilemma in which I found myself. Suppose you are at a large fair and outside one of the exhibits you come across a small child of four or five. He is crying, he is lost. You look around and can find no one who appears to be responsible for him. Through his tears he tells you that he was with his mother and that she has gone.

'"Gone! No, sweet, she must be here somewhere. Take my hand we will go and find the people who can put a message over the loudspeaker."

'He looks at you with trust but little comprehension. When you get to the central office he has stopped crying. He tells you his name and says that his mother was also crying when he last saw her. She had turned away from him, he says, and he had waited a long time but she had not returned. As the message is broadcast for the second time your stomach tightens. You have sensed the truth: the child has been abandoned. What you first thought, and told him, would be an easy operation has suddenly become dramatically more complex. His position, your position and his mother's position have altered dramatically in the story that, seconds before, was going to be solved within minutes.

'When my young patient first presented to me he gave a good account of himself and his background, but as that first interview progressed I realised, or did I just formulate, that he was in grave psychological danger. You may say in retrospect that I had two main options: to sit with him and assist him while he figured himself out, or to help him by showing him how things really were and what he needed to do to get himself out of danger. I judged then, and it may well have been a mistake, that I only really had the second option. He needed much more substantial help than at first appeared. I was also swayed I think by the fact that I understood his situation so well and thought that I would be a very good person to help him. I liked him! Isn't that the basis of a lot of good psychotherapy?'

The big question is, do I thank Dr Geering for saving me, or do I accuse her of holding me up – literally? Supposing Gloria were to have told me that I had, she was sure, the capacity to sort myself out and that part of that process was going to involve growing up and looking after the young boy in me who had been lost, and who required not her nurture but my own. Part of me believes, now, that I may well have been able to do this. Such an achievement would have profoundly altered the course of my life. I would almost certainly have done things I did not, and avoided other things I did. Would I have been happy? In many ways that is irrelevant. The point about that scenario is that I would have done developmentally appropriate tasks. Instead, in saving me, in holding me herself, Gloria perhaps perpetuated the life of the damaged child within me. I learnt, with her parenting, that there was much to be gained, particularly in the relationship with women, in continuing to ignore the child in me and instead have others look out for him in me. This made it more likely that I would run away from the home and homeland that was not working for me. Find and marry a person, who, like Gloria, could continue to instruct me in the ways of the world and in the ways of myself. In the process of leaving the young neglected boy to others it was psychologically impossible for the man to be a father.

So here I am, spectacularly out of date with my

development. And I am looking back to Gloria who saved me and held me up.

My writing teacher says that putting the self and the writing in the same place does something special and I think, without knowing it, she's referring to a sort of psychotherapy. She doesn't use the word 'healing', yet many references are made to writers who recovered themselves with the words they wrote. I have experienced this now. I call it the space that has opened up between the screen of my word processor and myself – my unnarrated memory of events and my experience of those events which unfurl in words on the screen. Unfurled, the heavy cord of emotion, all the feelings, now gently separated, the strands looped back to the place where they began, where they belong. Held together and yet distinct. I am no longer my story and this writing is not only pleasurable but healing.

    The writer benefits from writing and, if it's any good, the reader will benefit from it too. The psychotherapist benefits from providing psychotherapy and, if it's any good, the patient will too. There is a clue here for the psychotherapist and for the writer. If psychotherapy and writing are to be helpful and defining for the recipient they must hold the person in a tense and, for a time, uncomfortable position of statement without resolution. This will move the person on to something new. If it does this, the effects of the psychotherapy and of the reading will be permanent because it will have helped to define the person. W.H. Auden knew when he farewelled W.B. Yeats on the eve of the war, 'in the nightmare of the dark', that 'poetry makes nothing happen'.

Like psychotherapy it 'survives in the valley of its saying'. Gloria was the riverbanks wherein my isolation and griefs and raw beliefs could find a way of happening, a mouth.

At first she was like an encyclopaedia of the soul. Then slowly she became an encyclopaedia of *my* soul. But the legacy of her relationship with me, her method, has become over the years since our last meeting as powerful as the patterning of words flowing together, a poem.

hamlet

The prince prophesies our limits four centuries later, when any of us comes to realize that even enormous knowledge of our own consciousness is of little help in knowing what is not conscious, the mystery that baffles the will.
— Harold Bloom, How to Read and Why.

I

Hugh Huggett was a dour man, much too beaten down by life for his mid-thirties. His shoulders sloped from his neck, and his mouth was similarly sadly sloping. He spoke in an unattractive nasal tone from under his top lip and overbite. He wore the same green tweed jacket and knitted tie for as long as I knew him. The same tortoiseshell glasses too, which he fingered back onto his nose nervously.

'This term we study Shakespeare.'

It was a strange introductory comment to something which would take a lifetime to explore.

'The Matriculation Board has nominated *Hamlet* as this year's Shakespeare.'

This, mumbled into a cardboard box on his desk from which he was drawing handfuls of dusty, small, blue, hard-covered copies of *Hamlet*. I didn't realise then that he might as well have said: this term I will introduce you to psychology – the subject that I have studied all my life so far.

I am mystified by the size of the effect of those two terms we spent reading *Hamlet*. It started a process which continues now, a relationship not only with that play but with Shakespeare which I had no way of understanding or predicting at the time. Relationships which grow – so that as the individual changes, something new, something different is offered – are rare between people. For example, while I was introduced to the erotic possibilities of a woman in relation to Lyle, my girlfriend when I was seventeen, it was nevertheless with other women that this part of me flourished and matured. With Shakespeare the *same plays*, and in particular *Hamlet*, were there as my sense of myself and the world grew and changed. There was more of me to discover in Shakespeare as the years went on. Indeed, Hamlet himself grew in complexity to suit my development. And it is in knowing that this process is ongoing that a secure, almost contented, pleasure creeps over me today. It is a rewarding relationship one can trust whomever one might turn out to be.

I looked forward to those classes, reading *Hamlet*, with savour seldom rivalled in my secondary school education. What was it that appealed? I loved the idea of a play; I'd acted in several thus far in my school career. It was the idea of putting on an identity, experimenting with different ways of being a person, that attracted me to drama. I saw, even then, that Hamlet was a character who could be styled in various ways: the text interpreted like a musical score but with more freedom. I got the idea that one could try on Hamlet like a costume, see what one's personality did to the role; see what the role did to one's personality. What a fit we made: the play poised for interpretation; Hamlet poised for action; and me poised for life.

And I liked the words. While many in the class were complaining about the arcane and complicated language, I thrived on it. My copy of the play from that year still has neat synonyms written in the margins through much of the text. I loved finding out the meaning of new words and working out the meaning and the irony of clever phrases. I think I understood that more words meant more emotional colour, more opportunity for understanding. Of course the story of the troubled and troublesome Prince enthralled me too. I could identify with an emotional state of being angry with everyone, as I could with family turmoil and loss, and trouble with girls. But more than any other aspect of Hamlet's person, I could feel in myself a profound sense of waiting for something to happen, something which would clarify personal initiative which the whole audience of my life was waiting to see. I did not use Hamlet's dithering as a defence when others intruded on me with demands for action. I was not nearly that interpersonally skilled. I felt only a sense of camaraderie not *to* Hamlet but *from* him, in my sense of frustrated inaction.

There were many things I did not realise about Hamlet at the time. One of these is the notion that Hamlet, perhaps more than any other Shakespearian character, specialises in what Bloom refers to as 'self-overhearing'. We did look, in some detail, at the various soliloquies and their meaning, so I must have received a primitive idea about this 'self-overhearing' and what it was about. I could not have imagined, though, that it was to be the foundation of my professional life as a psychotherapist, a job which could so easily be defined as constructing, with others, 'self-overhearing' contexts. That it was a crucial function for the self, especially the troubled self, in search of healing. A self-recovering overhearing in the held presence of the therapy room. Not everyone can write down what they hear when they listen to themselves. But most people can speak what they hear in their heads and if the listening person provides first an audience, and then some useful questions, something quite transformative can occur. Make the listening person a psychologist and the process is called psychotherapy. That was to be my career. I wonder if I felt an inkling of it in the Shakespeare class? Or whether the Shakespeare class inkled it into my personality?

Bloom speaks of Hamlet's adept character analysis:

> ... everyone he speaks to in the play (except the Ghost) is clarified for us by Hamlet's questionings, even if he or she cannot accept self-clarification. Why read *Hamlet*? Because it will clarify the reader, if the reader can make that acceptance.

What would it be like to be confronted by Hamlet? Bloom asks:

Imagine that you are one of these 'attendant lords' with whom T.S. Eliot's J. Alfred Prufrock identifies: 'one that will do/ To swell a progress, start a scene or two.'

Hamlet *did* confront me when I was sixteen. I *was* an attendant lord. But it was initially more humiliating than enlightening.

It was my language disability again. Huggett was a bully, a sarcastic, critical man and I was a mildly troublesome sort of boy. The two went together.
    'Relph, why are you whistling in class?'
    'I'm happy, Sir.'
    'Well don't.'
    'Don't be happy, Sir?'
    'Don't whistle, Relph.'
    And barely audible: 'Why would a boy like you be happy anyway?'
    'Sir?'
    'Nothing Relph ... Everyone turn to Act 1 Scene 2; it's on page 78. We'll read the whole scene. Gould, you read Claudius King of Denmark; Smith, Gertrude the Queen.'
    A ripple of laughter.
    'Shhh! Fraser, Voltimand; Dell, Cornelius; Schoeman, Polonius; Austin, Laertes; Gillham, Hamlet; Relph, Others.'
    An eruption of laughter which, this time, was not checked. Beyond the slight that this was on me and my intelligence, for no distinction was being made between intelligence and attainment, it did me a favour: I was in the play and yet I was an observer. From that position Hamlet could work on

me, begin the long process of clarifying me.

'Others' was my vantage point from which I watched and listened to the action of the play and to the class discussion which followed. The process was self-clarifying to the extent that this is possible in early adolescence. It introduced me to the psychological conflicts within Hamlet and to the unfolding of relationships in the court. It advanced my skill at reading other people – their traits and the effect of these on other people. The specifics of the play made instant general connections in my emerging personality. I came to realise later that this is the genius of Shakespeare. The small metaphor in the line and the large metaphor in the play. Huggett the teacher, for all his mean shortcomings, somehow interested us in what was happening to Hamlet the individual. *He* asked us questions and in turn rewarded our questioning. Although he did not get us to learn the lines, they sounded so good that some of us repeated them to each other in our own small lunchtime soliloquies. We were indiscriminate, which is fine with Shakespeare. These word-parcels slowly seeped into my consciousness with an increasing fullness of meaning.

II

One Saturday morning thirty-four years after those classes, I discussed Hamlet with my psychotherapist. Or rather I overheard myself say:

'There is an indecision, an existential indecision which, if you are true to yourself and you don't submit to the clamour of others' views, is not resolvable merely by thinking about the problem. On the other hand, action – so prized by our society as a means of making a decision or getting unstuck – is also not a solution to this sort of indecision. That has been done to death, literally, by the French Existentialists amongst others. Hamlet is endlessly thoughtful. He talks to himself, which by the way is good for the audience, stuck with their own indecision. But the point is, it's meant to be good for Hamlet himself, this overhearing.

'That's what you're doing here with me. By giving me the time and space and then listening with some kind of warm and non-judgemental attention, we have a hope that, with the audience, the passive and sympathetic audience, I'll make sense of something and be able to move along with an aspect of my life. There are plenty of arguments these days for people just getting on with things and acting on the information they have to hand. It doesn't matter if they get things wrong, we all do; that's the argument. Well that's all very mediocre and fine for people, especially in the first half of their lives when they feel like there's plenty of time to put things right. But Hamlet is like a fifty year old really, he recognises that any decision he makes will have negative consequences.

'Hamlet is the opposite of a woman I was talking to recently, the wife of a friend of mine. She is nearing fifty and she clings to the appearance of classy, well-groomed success. Chanel sunglasses, you know. I asked her whether, like the rest of us getting to fifty, she'd been reviewing her life so far?

'"Yes" she said, "I have." There was a slightly different

tone in her voice at this point. A formality, like she was presenting something to an audience. She sounded rehearsed.

'"I look back on my life and can't believe how wonderful it's been."

'It would have been nice to think she meant this about life itself, but she was warming to her theme, and it was clear she was talking about herself.

'"I've worked in such interesting positions, like the one at the moment: the Women for World Peace and Freedom from Poverty Committee that I run. I meet the most interesting people. And we meet in great places like New York and Geneva. I've got some terrific friends; God my friends are good to me, I've been so lucky to have the friends I've had. Then there's my family, it's my proudest achievement to have raised the two boys." Somehow even this sounded like the *right* proudest achievement, very human, not very materialistic, selfless. I couldn't believe how it was all coming out like some kind of curriculum vitae, a presentation to some selection committee. I fully expected her to complete her answer to my innocent question with "and I play tennis and hold a current class A driver's licence". But it was worse than that, her presentation ended with: "Do you know what?"

'I couldn't think. She mimed thoughtfulness. "Do you know what? Looking back, I can't think of a single thing I would do differently."'

Looking up, I saw that my therapist was still attending in spite of my monologue. She understood the Shakespeare thing and psychotherapy much better than Gloria would have. Just give Hamlet the audience and let him try to figure it out; it doesn't have to be a conversation. Or maybe it does have to be a conversation, but one where one person listens a lot more than usual and one talks a lot more than usual. With Gloria I'd had to do most of the listening, which, like my first reading of Hamlet, was probably appropriate for that time in my development.

'You can imagine how this woman's words affected me,' I said. 'Knowing as you do that there is hardly a thing I can think of that I would do the same if I had my time over again.'

I didn't wait for a commentary but went on: 'Lots of men seem to have this Hamlet indecision about their relationships in the middle of their lives. On the surface of things Hamlet's main indecision seems to be whether or not to avenge his father's murder by killing his uncle. How to do that right; how to get the timing right. But he's also stuck between his mother and Ophelia. No one is really free to love someone while they're still psychologically busy with someone else. Clara knows that in *Sons and Lovers* when she more or less hands Paul back to Miriam. She knows Paul's love of anyone is doomed because he hasn't disengaged himself from his mother.'

I paused at this point to let the psychotherapist do her job. I thought she would have led the way with something like: 'And you? Do you think you're disengaged enough from your relationship with your mother, or do you think that holds you back too?' She didn't, so I went on to answer it anyway. Hamlet in full soliloquy.

'Hamlet turns out to be such a superb example for men

and for me, precisely because it's his mother he hasn't come away from psychologically. That and the fact that his connection to her is represented by anger and rage, not by apparent love. You don't necessarily look for such a regressed psychological state in someone as old as fifty, but Hamlet's a young man, you would look for that in him; though it's often so disguised in that age group because they are so bound up with their girlfriends or wives who are often being mothers to them. A man is never too young or too old to look for clues to his psyche in his relationship with his mother.' I paused.

'Take the guy I was talking to the other day. He's fifty, his birthday was just last month. He got two clear statements in the card from his mother. First she said that she was sorry that she hadn't been there for him emotionally when he was younger. That felt good to him because something he'd always felt as a lack had been validated from the very person in question. The second thing she told him was that she recalled with pleasure what a wonderful experience it had been watching him grow through his boyhood.'

I was giving it to her on a plate but she just smiled and let me carry on doing the work myself. God how different psychotherapy was from physiotherapy. (This is the problem Andrew, this is the reason Andrew, this is the answer Andrew, these are the exercises Andrew.)

Again I was struck by how different this was from the way it had been with Gloria as a nineteen year old. She had clearly been a mother and a father to me; but that was not required now.

'Perhaps my anger towards my mother does indeed stop

me from fully committing myself to a relationship with a woman now that I'm finally psychologically independent. Now that I don't really need a woman, my anger to my mother can be the thing to keep me from fully relating. The shroud of protection. The shroud of perfection. Before, when I needed a woman, the need kept me in the relationship and kept my eye off my mother and my unresolved hatred of her. If she wrote me a card with that stuff in it I would be instantly suspicious. I'd examine the pen marks on the paper to see if there were any clues she was insincere; that's a form of holding on, really.

'So, what if Hamlet presented for psychotherapy? Would you just let him soliloquise?' Now I was complicating things, but she smiled, she loved the complications; she was bored with psychiatry and she hankered after the more thought-provoking. In spite of herself, she leaned slightly forward in her chair and a skein of hair, always decorously and tightly ponytailed, fell across her face and she smoothed it behind her ear with her hand open to me. My entertainment continued, centre stage.

'Perhaps one wouldn't let him just ramble on, one soliloquy after another. Perhaps it would be time for some more advice.' I didn't wait for her agreement.

'From what you've said, Hamlet, you can't clearly work out how awful your mother is. There have been plenty of loving and warm aspects to your relationship with her, but now, just as you're forming your definitive view of yourself in relation to others – and in particular to your father and your mother – she is implicated in the death of your father. Like most young men you feel appropriately shocked by your mother's mistreatment of your father as well as her unfaithfulness to him. This is because it reflects on your mother's relationship with you as well. You can't trust that she has been a good mother to *you* all these years if this is how it turns out in relation to your father and, by implication, to you. But your mother keeps feeding you lines about her gullibility and naivety and this brings forward a protectiveness in you. Maybe she's just been unwise, not unloving. If only you could tell what is the real woman, you would know how to act. But the problem is you feel this ambiguity in your relationship with her and it robs you of being able to take decisive action in relation to your uncle, and also inhibits the development of a relationship with Ophelia who is equally puzzling as a woman, especially now that others are dissuading her from a relationship with you.

'I suggest you get on and kill your uncle at the next opportunity and kick your mother out of the court and get on with the business of being king of Denmark. Now is the time to do this; don't think any more about it. Ophelia and the rest of the court will respect your decisiveness and all will be back to normal in a year or so. Then you can make a difference by having a different relationship with Ophelia, or whomever you choose, than the one your father had with your mother which was clearly problematic and which they did nothing to improve. And, by the way, the one person you've told me about in all this who you feel you can really trust – that Horatio fellow. Yes, I believe you're right: he is to be trusted. But more than that, use your relationship with him to build up your trust in yourself. It's true what you said about there being nothing either good or bad but thinking makes it so. Go on now and fix things up in your self; let your mother go; make a happy and meaningful relationship with a woman and you will be able to defend your country adequately against people like the Norwegians.'

The session was at an end; I had kept an eye on the time; she didn't even have that responsibility. She just smiled, she seemed lost in thought but that was not my responsibility. She focused her eyes onto the clock and a slight tremor of her head suggested she'd been a captive audience. She smiled again and said yes she'd see me in two weeks time.

III

So Hamlet stayed with me, as Horatio did with him, a sort of psychological companion, a reflective and yet very human surface. At one stage, his heroic refusal to make a decision in the face of apparently shifting moral ground appealed to me; at another, his complete inability to take initiative, his purposefulness quite incapacitated, resonated with my state: ... *the native hue of resolution / ... sicklied o'er with the pale cast of thought*. I too experienced his sane madness as he went around the court alienating himself from everyone. I felt at times the same carelessness of his own fate, his dense unhappiness with himself and the world.

Don't get this wrong, I did not sit down and re-read *Hamlet* every time I got in a fix, though this would seem like a very good thing for any man to do. It was mostly much more incidental than that. A tract of iambic pentameter would pop into my head and I would follow it back to its emotional meaning. 'Why am I saying this bit of Shakespeare to myself, like a song stuck in my head?' Sometimes it was a big one like:

> What's Hecuba to him, or he to her,
> That he should weep for her? What would he do
> Had he the motive and the cue for passion
> That I have? He would drown the stage with tears,
> And cleave the general ear with horrid speech,
> Make mad the guilty and appal the free,
> Confound the ignorant, and amaze indeed
> The very faculties of eyes and ears.

If I checked the text, I might have bits wrong but there it was, a sense of a state which was consoling because someone before had tracked it down so perfectly.

Sometimes it would be a small one like: *This is I, Hamlet the Dane*. Although I've always said, 'Tis I, Hamlet the Dane.'

What's all that about? Is it too minor, too superficial to make any sense out of? Perhaps so. But if I had been wondering about my sense of identity all that week, or if I'd finally sensed my emotional commitment to a cause, perhaps not.

And it was the psychotherapist in me, who – though never far away from the particularities of the problems and the processes in *Hamlet* and in the other plays – nevertheless learnt more from Shakespeare about the process of change itself and the way in which reflection lies at its centre, than from all the books I read on psychotherapy together.

Then again, it was within the psychotherapy room that I encountered both in myself as patient, and in those who came to see me, the limitations of what we know, our psychological theory and the importance of recognising that limitation. It can be disrespectful to apply a simple theory to life and to the person's experience of it. In those moments of the unmeasurable and the unexplainable, literature has aided my interactions with others more than psychological theory. This too can be found in the *secular scripture,* as Harold Bloom admiringly refers to the complete human coverage of the works of Shakespeare:

> *There are more things in heaven and earth, Horatio,*
> *Than are dreamt of in your philosophy.*

my mother's book

Those who know ghosts tell us that they long to be released from their ghost life and led to rest as ancestors.
— Hans Loewald, *Papers on Psychoanalysis*

When I was in my late childhood my mother used to refer to a book that she had written. She said it was called *Grey Gull's Feather* and from the little she said about it I assumed it was a tragic love story. Back then I wanted to read it very badly but she didn't offer it and I wouldn't have had the verbal facility to get through it anyway. That she didn't read it to me is perhaps a sign of maternal protection of my vulnerable emotional state at the time since it would almost certainly have been a thinly disguised rendition of her relationship, however fanciful, with a man who was not my father. The more prosaic and probably more realistic reason she didn't read it to me might have been because the whole thing was a secret from her jealous and unstable husband. She did tell me, without much sense of outrage, that a publisher had turned it down.

Grey Gull's Feather was written in longhand on sheets of quarto paper. She had written it with a fountain pen and Quink royal blue ink. The pages were tied up with thin blue ribbons between two sheets of card. It smelt of naphthalene and was stored in a particular place in our house, I think I knew where, but it seems in my memory to be a place I rarely ever got access to. I never had any thought at all of reading it on the quiet, which probably meant that place was locked.

Occasionally throughout my childhood my mother would mention the book to me like a guilty secret. I wouldn't be surprised if none of my siblings knew about it. There was a sort of illicit privilege that went with the knowledge.

When she was eighty I brought the book up in conversation without using the title.

'Oh yes,' she confirmed, 'I did write a book, but I never had any idea of publishing it. It was pretty terribly written. Just did it for myself really, something I had to get out.'

'And where is it now?' enquired my partner, with licence I didn't have.

'You know, I don't know,' she said, with the kind of minute and convoluted dishonesty that had characterised her communication for as long as I could remember. There was a pause. More information was required.

'I think I must have thrown it out ages ago, probably when I left Clarence. Yes I would think it was when I left Clarence. But you know it was never for keeping or for other people, just something I had to get out, and when it was done I could leave it behind.'

An awkward silence. I looked at Rebecca and she at me. You can't really proceed with a conversation which everyone knows is dishonest; there doesn't seem any point. It was my mother's way of killing a conversation, killing a relationship. Perhaps the book had been about the death of a relationship, one which had shocked her so badly that even writing about it had not given her the courage to open her heart like that again.

There are few clues, but then the real events upon which the book was written were probably very slim too. Which is not to minimise their significance. Relationship can be like stem-cells or DNA: a small bit can encode a lot of meaning, meaning which can go on generating itself as time goes on. In the absence of any facts, I did spend a little time imagining my mother's book. A Georgette Heyer-like novel of driving sentiment rather than accomplished writing. A plot in which love is pledged, a token is given and the tragedy of a young sailor's life sacrificed in the Mediterranean Sea. The pain of loss is somehow construed as a gift when the young woman who is left behind realises that spiritual fulfilment is more important than the evanescence of relationship. The strange echo of all this had been transmitted when my mother read me Paul Gallico's *The Snow Goose* when I was six or seven. For some years after that, I had listened to the dramatised recording of it again and again as if to purge *myself* of some tragedy I did not know about.

Forty years on from when I first became interested in *Grey Gull's Feather*, my mother gave me another book which she had written. A book without a title. A book about her life and ancestry which started with her paternal great-grandfather and ended at the start of her adult life, with the death, in the Second World War, of the man who she wanted to marry. As soon as I paged through the densely handwritten book I felt a familiarity, not in the prose but in the look and feel of the writing. Here it was again, though this time the blank quarto paper was bound into a journal with a cover depicting semiprecious stones and three trilobites grouped together as if they had been washed up on a beach somewhere. The royal blue ink created a smart look of contrast with the unlined, bleached paper. The handwriting looked identical to the writing I remembered all those years before.

This was a much more significant piece of writing to me than I could have imagined my mother's novel to have been.

My mother's life contained four major tragedies. They defined her. The first two, like her longitude, marked the beginning and the end of her childhood. The second two were in her adulthood; like her latitude they confined her to a narrow band in which she felt some safety. It seems to me those impacts on a life that occur in childhood, and over which we have little control, set up, if we do nothing about them, the way in which later impacts confine our adulthood. These first two calamities were written down, albeit glancingly, in this handwritten account of her life up until the age of twenty.

My mother was born into a family of five. Her parents lived on a plantation in the subtropical coastal bush of Natal in South Africa. Reen, as her mother was called, had come from England as a twenty year old to be a governess for her young cousin, and had fallen in love with and married his older brother. The couple had three children in a short time. Things were looking okay until Reen got pregnant for the fourth time: twins were born, and it seemed to usher in a change in the fortune of the family. The little boy of the pair was unwell from the start. No one was quite sure what was wrong with him and the doctor that did see him seemed to reassure them that little Jack would be all right in the long run. By comparison his twin sister, my mother, seemed robust but it wasn't clear then, with all the worry about Jack, that she was not in particularly good health either.

That year of my mother's birth, her father Harold had fallen out with his two younger brothers with whom he farmed. There are no details of this recorded by my mother except that it was to do with the inheritance of the land from their father. Whatever the dispute, the outcome seemed clear: Harold no longer felt he would get ahead by staying on the farm.

The need to get ahead came in the same year. The twins were barely six weeks old. My grandfather and his brothers had gone to the pub in the seaside village a few miles from the farm. The details of this event are sketchy too but in the course of the evening a man who they hardly knew cast aspersions on my grandmother. Now that I think of it, he could have said something like: 'Harry, you don't have any sisters to fuck, so you fuck your cousin.' Whatever the insult, my grandfather, who could box a bit, landed some heavy blows and before the men were separated, the offender's nose and cheekbone were broken. The police were involved and a court case ensued which resulted in my grandfather having to pay a sizeable fine. His brothers would not lend him the money and so he took his savings and moved his new family a hundred and twenty kilometres to the south where there was a plantation of trees for sale. A reasonable profit was to be had by organising the cutting and transporting of this timber to the growing town of Durban. So Harold purchased the trees and prepared to cut them down and have them picked up by sailing ship. The operation would take most of the spring and go on into the summer; by autumn the timber would be on the way to market. Then the fine could be paid and new ventures could be undertaken. 'Don't fret, my love,' Harold would say to Reen. 'You'll see our ship will come in.'

The small clearing in the forest across the Mzimvubu River, in a place they called Pondoland after the indigenous people, was not a place to raise infants. Reen had predicted that the change might do Jack's breathing good but the frail baby was often blueish around the mouth. He didn't feed well and his breathing was laboured. The doctor who they consulted again before leaving the farm said there was nothing that could be done for the boy, he was on his own now and might well survive. In any case, the nearest hospital was two days away by horse at Port Shepstone.

A few months after arriving in the clearing where Harold had erected a small timber cabin, Jack died. Later the timber was loaded onto the *S.S. Frontier* which, that same night, went down in a terrible storm and the entire cargo of livestock and timber was lost.

The story is told in my mother's memoir with the characteristic combination of sentimental detail and piety which she often brought to bear on subjects of great emotional import:

> *Although I don't know the actual date of Jack's death, I do know that he was about seven and a half months old, so it must have been in the middle of March 1927, so the* Frontier *was probably wrecked fairly soon afterwards. Because my parents did not believe in Infant Baptism, the local Church of England minister could not bury my twin brother and a messenger had to be dispatched to a Methodist Mission about 80 miles away to make arrangements for the interment. Dad made the little coffin, and the sad task of nailing on the lid was alleviated by an elderly woman who lived close by. She saw what was happening and came and took the hammer from him and completed the task herself. Somehow the Pharisaical attitude of the priest was at least partially redeemed by the loving ministry of the 'good Samaritan' lady.*

She goes on:

> *When I was about eleven Dad and Gladys and I went to Port St Johns on our way to East London by car. I was rather overawed by the denseness of the forest and the primitiveness of the house that Dad pointed out as 'possibly' being the one we had lived in. In spite of not having known all the modern comforts and conveniences at the time,*

life for Mum and Dad must have been tough – really tough. They had no hot water laid on; no refrigeration; no electric light; no water-borne sanitation. No money, and five growing children. When we visited Port St Johns and tried to find our old home in the forest, we also went to the cemetery and found the numbered stake in a grave which identified it as Jack's. It was overgrown with weeds and grass, and Dad wept a bit and I felt very sad that life had been so hard for them, but I think we felt it best not to mark the little grave in any way. Jack's short life had left its benediction and its pain, and our visit seemed to bring some 'closure' for Dad. I've always been glad that I saw the significant landmarks of the time, but am not unhappy that the grave remains unmarked. The little boy's life was engraved on the hearts of his parents, and Margaret and Aubrey both remember him. His task was completed.

History is interpreted, especially personal history, with the kind of psychological insight that can only arise long after the events have been lived out. Many people cannot feel adequately for the experiences of others, but just as many can feel too much for the experiences of others, especially those who they are close to. How can I understand this, the first of my mother's four tragedies? What emptiness did it leave in her early life? What grief in the people who were caring for her as she survived and grew? Was the resoluteness of her mother and father's position as they faced up to the days following the death and the shipwreck an indication of how emotions would be dealt with? Was any other emotional style possible? How does the retrospective religious gloss given to the events in the writing fit with my mother's earlier profound sadness at eleven? And was that sadness really about the hard time her parents had had or was she experiencing the grief that had been stored up in all of them for years?

The same religious gloss is there again in the second tragedy which concluded my mother's childhood. Now a seventeen year old in the last year of school, she was in love with a handsome English sailor. Even then she knew that John, who had promised to return, was the man for her. The account of her ancestry and young life ends with these words:

> *The giant, camouflaged battleship was, eventually, restored to naval glory and, in spite of the usual secrecy surrounding the movement of shipping, John was able to 'warn' us of their sailing a few days in advance. At Durban Girls' High we had an assembly each morning, and announcements were made about girls whose brothers or dads had been killed in action, and we sang a hymn and a prayer was said and a short portion of scripture was read.*
>
> *'Eternal Father Strong to Save' took on new meaning for me.*
>
>   *O hear us when we cry to Thee*
>   *For those in peril on the sea*
>
> *I wanted John to be safe with all my heart.*
>
>   *From rock and tempest, fire and foe,*
>   *Protect them where so ere they go.*

I had yet to learn that to trust for something is not as satisfying as to trust in Someone. I trusted God for John's safety, but I had yet to recognise that it is safer far to trust in the ultimate loving purpose of an all-wise God who can do no wrong. John was a wireless telegraphist on HMS Barham, *and was on duty when the ship was sunk on 25th November 1941 with great loss of life.*

A single concluding paragraph reads:

From all my tentative looking out on the world in Bloem, and all my expanded learning and crossing of new thresholds in Maritzburg, I had graduated at Vause Road to the ranks of those who have experienced love and death and sorrow and was, inexorably on the road to adulthood.

In the lines of my mother's book, I at last read the defining parameters of her emotional life. Her book was a gift to me of many layers, most precious of these an understanding of her limitations and how they had been formed. To put one's parents on the analyst's couch is an important part of one's psychological development and it was my mother's writing which was so valuable in this endeavour.

I could understand why my boy tears would be elicited again and again when I heard the story of *The Snow Goose* first from my mother's reading and later from my own reading of the slim text. *Grey Gull's Feather*, *The Snow Goose,* and my mother's grief were inseparable. And at least in the first fifteen years of my life I was inseparable from them. Now the blue ink on the page of the book she wrote for me seems indistinguishable from the book she wrote for herself forty-five years before. And the grief of the first two tragedies of her life seems to mingle with the grief of the second two in which I shared.

It was in reading first, and latterly in writing, that I experienced the emotional world and began an understanding of it. My mother, with all her emotional deficiencies, was there teaching me to read by reading to me and perhaps she taught me the value of writing too. Both reading and writing were means to an end and ends in themselves.

The child grows up to become the parent in the family of literature. I imagine Shakespeare reading Chaucer; Milton reading Shakespeare; Blake reading Milton; Wordsworth reading Blake. I imagine Sterne reading Swift; Lawrence reading Hardy; Woolf reading Dickens; Hemingway reading Conrad. An evolving conversation over centuries.

These things are written down so that the lonely tears of all our grief can find consolation in the grief of others. So that our lives might not, as my mother's was, be described by grief, but instead reach outwards, from the longitude of childhood trauma to as wide a latitude as we are. Why then would we dilute our tears with empty promises? Why set them aside, behind pious lessons? False hope would seem to kill the consolation that is felt when the lined and tender hand of understanding reaches across generations, sometimes centuries, to indicate that one is not alone in one's sadness.

being herzog

Not that long disease, my life, but that long convalescence, my life.

— Saul Bellow, *Herzog*.

I

I was fifty when I read Saul Bellow's *Herzog*, the age where the dual functions of literature – consolation and identity – unbalance again, and books appear to push past issues of identity towards a more exclusive meaning in the consolation they can offer. Whatever my experience, as a younger man, of the sensation of literature's understanding voice, it was now surpassed by Bellow's accurate reading of me. But I played a part in this. I was no longer looking for people I could emulate. Rather, it seemed, I was taken up with the task of coming to terms with the person I had turned out to be. Not that I regarded my identity with any satisfaction or sense of completeness. But I had not given up on the future – just on one of its more ambitious hopes:

myself. Whence do we arrive at the promise of a solution to our selves? How deeply is it etched into the collective mind that we will someday be completed, resolved, fully made? How long are we distracted by this quest? Now, at last, what I may become was not the big question. It had been replaced by: who I was and how I might relate to the world that I found myself within.

In this state I felt a haunting camaraderie with Herzog's self-examination:

> ... he admitted that he had been a bad husband – twice. Daisy, his first wife, he had treated miserably. Madeleine, his second, had tried to do him in ... To his own parents he had been an ungrateful child. To his country, an indifferent citizen. To his brothers and his sister, affectionate but remote. With his friends, an egotist. With love, lazy. With brightness, dull. With power, passive. With his own soul, evasive.

Not that Herzog's critical reflections were exactly mine, though they were close enough for me to worry about a syndrome. It was more the process of self-critical reflection that I recognised. Nor were these incisive commentaries, either in Herzog or in me, confined to the self. A running commentary, an obsessive note-writing to those who should take note, was there as well. Like Herzog, I too had recently felt that the only way to deal with the psychotic-like pressure of threatened disintegration was to write. To write one's observations was to provide a safe distance from the painfulness of things. An overhearing of oneself, this time –

a written plea. Was it disintegration that was threatening? Like Herzog's, my ego was basically intact; real psychosis was unlikely. But in this sensitised state, a sort of anti-autistic state, the world, especially the interpersonal world, could feel dangerously sharp, explosive, toxic, choking.

There are a number of psychological theories about this movement towards a more realistic view of oneself and one's place in the world. But they are usually convoluted and overdeveloped, as if the authors themselves were keen to explain how well-developed their own minds were.

Psychotherapists like me are often consulted by people who have just arrived at this point of recognition. The hoped-for way things might turn out to be is never going to happen. Indeed, no outcome is ever going to free them from the dreary responsibility for their own lives. In this state there is a realisation that their parents will never recognise who they really are. A man or a woman will never complete their incompleteness. A child or a fortune will never give the deserved respect. In the grief and sadness which accompanies this recognition, the psychotherapist is often a silent witness who seldom has to point out that the process is also one of liberation. The end of some of the worry of being in the world, yet the continuation of all the effort it requires. The transformation of guilt and blame into responsibility.

These two positions, freedom and responsibility, are not so much points on a line of a journey through life, but places one visits repeatedly in the endless double helix of life. William Blake understood this before psychiatry got involved. There is innocence, he said, and there is experience; but experience is gained only to visit innocence again – innocence regained through experience. Herzog understands this; it's why he answers his concerned Dr Emmerich's offer to recommend a psychiatrist with: *No, I've had all the psychiatry I can use.*

The psychology theories had told me all this; a single line of Bellow showed me. It was with relief and recognition that I read one of the great opening lines of American literature: *If I am out of my mind, it's all right with me, thought Moses Herzog.*

Here was the germ again. I couldn't have articulated my immediate knowledge that this book was to be about a man in the middle of his life coming to terms with who he was, resisting the definitions of the world, and facing life and death with as much clarity as one person is capable of, but I knew that the book was for me to read now. And within the first few pages I had confirmation: Bellow had read the dilemmas of middle age, of failure and survival, and had put it down in such a way as to offer a very different person on a different continent at a different period in history consolation and comfort.

Reading Herzog offered me no direction. I was in search of none, just the companionship of being got. A hand on the shoulder, a nod, a wry smile and 'I know.' This knowledge is subtly reassured by the absence of quotation marks in the opening line. The narrator, Bellow, is reading Herzog's mind, being his psychotherapist. And he is letting me overhear the process. Herzog has come to terms with the peculiarity of himself, he is rising above the demands of social convention. He is developing a deeper security in the self; promise has lessened and unpaid-for emotion is absent. I did not ask myself if I thought the same or felt the same as Herzog; the experience was more one of reassurance.

Years before, the opening line of *Moby-Dick* had summoned me to a very different experience: *Call me Ishmael*. The sentence beckoned to everything ahead. I will take you places and show you things which every man must come to terms with, which every man must be amazed by and survive. I will get in closer to you, dear Reader, than you expected. Above all else you can trust me to be your guide in some rough sailing ahead. That first chapter was called 'Loomings'.

I needed Ishmael at nineteen, needed him again in my early thirties, but at fifty I needed Herzog.

Shortly after my first encounter with Bellow's writing, I wrote the following dysphoric entry in my journal. When I had finished writing it I uncharacteristically gave the entry a title: *Being Herzog*.

> *Like Herzog I could not stop the self-reflection. The constant commentary which murmured on somewhere in my mind. What was the process? Mind was ever vigilant to the things requiring comment. Waiting like an angry cat, crouched, ready to unwind with claw and snarling tooth. Was it that, or was it the other way around, where the commentary in my mind bent whatever was presented to me to its own dyspeptic purposes? Since the argument of the moment always found such easy example everywhere I*

looked, I had begun to suspect myself. That would be more like my father who had warped reality, bent it to fit his mind, skewed the interpersonal space. I needed Herzog's clarity as I walked out of the front door, perhaps too receptive, on this opaline morning where the sun was just hot in the milky blue sky of early spring.

The dogs, on my left, were eager to get going, straining on the leash. My neighbour across the street chose today to greet me; he hardly ever did. Though I stopped politely to exchange greetings, I despised the man and his family who had, the previous year, purchased and then razed a perfectly decent nineteen-thirties house together with its garden, its trees. In its place they had built a kitsch, low-slung house out of pale, pre-formed, synthetic look-like-limestone blocks with a sharply reflecting steel roof. This is what I had distastefully accustomed to as the view from my front door as I ventured into the world every day.

'A nice morning for gardening,' I said to the man in the parachute tracksuit and weekend stubble wielding a rake under newly planted saplings.

'Get this finished and then it's round the back to get that garden done.'

'What do you plan to do out the front here?'

'Well ... continue the blue and white theme,' he said, pointing educationally to the house. Couldn't miss that, old boy, I thought, these pale concrete blocks, the white framed bargain doors and the paint-box blue wooden eaves. But 'blue and white theme'? Sounds a little self-important, a touch overstated, don't you think? You're not exactly Josiah Wedgwood, though perhaps your wife thinks you are, or *perhaps she thinks she is and you're just doing what you're told and expecting people to be impressed by her ideas?* Instead I said, 'Hm?' and as one of the dogs sniffed my neighbour's leg I realised his tracksuit was in the blue and white theme too. I regretted putting that question mark in the pause in our interaction because my neighbour was leaning back on his heels preparing further instruction, this time in gardening.

'So, hence ... the silver birch trees. Over there, some garden beds with blue arums, and by the path some standard roses.' Ah! what a sensible choice, birch trees from the cold damp Siberian plains, here in semi-desert Western Australia where the dry salt wind rips and stains and kills anything tender on forty degree days. Would all four be dead by the middle of summer? And blue arums? He must mean agapanthus surely. Neighbour had looked up and down the street to demonstrate what he'd meant but not seeing what he was after left his ignorant student in the dark. Standard roses? My heart sank the most at this. They weren't going to be blue! No, they would be icebergs. Forty-five dollars each at the local garden centre, about as interesting and aesthetically pleasing as Weet-bix.

My dismay was partly because it completed the picture of mediocrity, but also because, with a stab of memory, I pictured the beautiful orange heritage rose which had stood in the centre of the old garden, nurtured for seventy years. I had thought about digging it up when the plan to destroy the house and garden had become obvious. The morning I'd planned to do it, I'd been woken by the seismic grumble of earth-moving equipment. I'd hurried over to save the plant but already it lay crushed and dismembered. Dead with no recognition but mine of a life spent in seventy spring blossomings and summer fragrances.

I could say nothing but clear my throat. But my neighbour was going on, warming to his theme.

'Round the back we'll have all the usual things. Fruit trees, a wall, a sunken garden behind the rather extensive alfresco,' he used the word as a noun, 'and,' a reverent pause, 'a water feature.'

No, he was not mocking himself. He was seriously committed to this vision. My head swimming Herzog-like again, I scoured the statement for any vestiges of sarcasm, even irony. Yet even that phrase, 'all the usual things' was utterly devoid of a point of view outside the self and its satisfied picture of the world. A shopping-list garden after the shopping-list house. Incapable of absorbing more of this, I started walking on just as my neighbour started complaining about the cost of getting a bobcat in to do the landscaping.

'It costs a fortune and half the time they don't even pitch up when they say they will,' he said, his voice rising to my back and the dogs' tails.

Since I couldn't stop the analysis and the commentary, I could not afford to hear any more from this man. As I walked on I tried to let the words drop away. It was a conscious effort not to absorb any more of this interaction. Still, it lurked dimly in my mind until the next snippet of human interaction slammed into me halfway through the long walk through the cemetery.

A family group was coming towards me – a mother, father and three children. The eldest, a girl of fifteen, eyed me and the dogs from some way off and as they passed she exclaimed delightedly:

'I want a dog like that, Mummy.' It was an excited comment which needed to be indulged. But the mother's cold, set face was unresponsive to her daughter's warmth and she wasn't going to miss an opportunity for behavioural commentary on this, her main rival in the world:

'Well! And what? You'd walk them everyday like that would you?'

The daughter was snuffed out, her enthusiasm killed in the graveyard. The coup de grace was a snort of humorous derision from the father. A short bitter sound which roughly translated as: 'You're fat, you're lazy and you don't know anything about the world.'

Even as my commentary about this interaction began, I was onto myself, as a sentence from *Herzog* I'd read before setting out on my walk, intruded: *You must aim the imagination also at yourself, point-blank.*

So how is it that you feel so indulgent of this young woman and her fantasy about the dog? Suddenly so accepting, compared to your neighbour and his mediocre, style-tragic images? Is it purely because they're your dogs and you think she has good taste to want a dog like Fergus and Rififi?

But it was deeper than that. I would not pin that on

myself. No, it was that fifteen year olds had a right to imagination, to fantasies about how they would like life to be. I did not hold them responsible for the impulsivity of their style nor even for its subservience to fashion. So what was the difference between the scorn I felt for my neighbour's ignorance and this girl's parents' scorn of her? Kids are meant to dream and adults are not; and if they do, they must at least do so with a little hint of self-reflection. It was fine that fifteen year olds said what they imagined the future to be like; they should not be held to account for that future. They were practising with many ideas and all of them ought be encouraged and given room for that, rather than punished. But forty year olds should know a thing or two by now and shouldn't go around spending money thoughtlessly or knocking down roses and houses just because they could afford to. Shouldn't go around erecting cheap and vulgar castles in Wedgwood.

If it had been my house, I mused, I'd have renovated, polished the floorboards, even built on in a sympathetic style out the back. I ruefully assumed that the big old fig tree was gone from the back garden. The previous neighbour had given me a shopping bag full of the delicious black and crimson fruit each summer.

And the young woman – I decided if I were her parent, I'd have stopped with her and admired the dogs. Said I agreed how beautiful they were. And as they'd walked on, the dogs and striding owner turning the corner, I'd have put my arm round my precious offspring and said: 'But not as beautiful as you, my Sasha.'

11

Well, they weren't going to accept me at Varuna. They'd turned down my application for a writing scholarship. Told me I shouldn't be put off: only six places were awarded; many outstanding applications; encouraged to apply for other grants soon to become available. But I didn't feel like it. I was not an Olympic champion. It was not just that people's bodies started giving out at thirty, this was not the only reason there were no Olympic champions of substantial age. It was also because people lost the determination and the daring; the great accompaniments to clarity of purpose. Instead I was filled with indecision and self-doubt. Where had that capacity gone, that fearless belief in my purpose? And why had I not put it to better use by making something to transcend and sustain?

Although the purpose had gone, my narcissism lingered and this proved to be a troubling combination. The truly committed narcissist, like my father, remains purposeful about the future. They put off ageing, refuse to look death in the face, keep planning with a kind of expectant immortality. Only at work could I still garner any sort of purpose about the future – mostly other people's. If I had been truly accepting of this state of affairs I would have felt the kind of peaceful resignation I had noted in my older friends who accommodated their age and failing capacity. But that past belief in myself was still there and its juxtaposition with the emptiness of old age staring me in the face, just a few years away, led me into frequent bouts of angriness during the day and at night. *The strength of Herzog's constitution worked obstinately against his hypochondria.* Oh! the nights were the worst. Then, a kind of swelling existential anxiety that everyone associated with being seventeen possessed my thoughts. Over and over the dilemmas and with them the realisation there was no time to resolve them, played like a distant soundtrack, perhaps Enya, with haunting yet indistinct lyrics. From nights like that, I would emerge slowly, eyes red and bulging, a fragile misgiving about the day and yet a knowledge that to get up and get out there was the only viable option. By ten or eleven a.m. I had listened to the stories of three or four patients. There was an apparent and ironic usefulness in this which led to a mild warming to life. It was like those days which dawned with a low fog hanging over the cemetery where I walked the dogs but which progressed quickly to a clear fresh morning with the first hour or two of sunshine. So, by lunchtime on most days I was feeling a distance from the existential angst of the night and was going about my day with a practised and carefully monitored program of activities. Clear air over acres of gravestones. But occasionally the doubts and fears of the night clouded my mind, especially when I had any time to myself, and left days overcast.

Thus caught between the night and the day; the pressure of other people, but also their distraction; the longing for time alone but the overwhelming and threatening thoughts that went with it; the failure of purpose, yet clinging to the sense of self by which I seemed to be maintaining life itself, I went on with the existence.

In his posture of collapse on the sofa, arms abandoned over his head and legs stretched away, lying with no more style than a chimpanzee, his eyes with greater than normal radiance watched his own work in the garden with detachment, as if he were looking through the front end of a telescope at a tiny clear image.

That suffering joker.

III

One cannot feel motivated to write after an afternoon reading Saul Bellow. His prodigious discipline and extraordinary capacity to capture in words what one has felt, thought and smelt, drains from one's imagination the idea that one may, oneself, be a writer. Mere conceit. Nothing to say that has not been said more skilfully, more eloquently. Some phrases left me unable to read on; made me want to adopt one of those Herzog couch-poses: *his arms rising behind him, his legs extended without aim.* Made me want to steady myself with a hand on the table or gaze unseeing at the ceiling or out of the window; drew me in so close that I wondered who this person was who had been listening in to my fears. Listening in with the same strange mixture of indulgence and criticism.

Take for example: *Not everyone threatened with a crackup can manage to go to Europe for relief.*

Or: *Indignation is so wearing that one should reserve it for the main injustice.*

Or: *He had been hoping for some definite sickness which would send him to a hospital for a while.*

Every few pages, the shock of recognition, an incisive observation thrown down, almost incidentally, along the path of the story of Herzog. I closed the book tight on the concert advertisement and gauged it from the side. One tenth read! The way my mind was exercised, I might have just finished reading a large novel. This was going to be an Atlantic crossing. I reckoned that I would break off from time to time to anchor myself, to take stock. Stop the words from taking over. I had often experienced that in the cinema where the pictures threatened to be too invasive. There, in the darkened theatre, the green glow of the exit sign above the door offered reassurance of the outside world to where one might escape. With Bellow I had to snap the book shut and toss it carelessly to one side. If I treated it like the grenade it was and handled it with care, I feared that, like fears themselves, I might give it even more power and fall further under its spell.

Yet my mind was sometimes not on Herzog as much as it was on Bellow. The greater, yet less defined, presence. The store from which Herzog had been constructed. The image of Bellow I was growing in my mind was constructed by the rendering of this main character – Herzog. See how the words speak for themselves? That, and the details of the man from Martin Amis in *Experience*. Amis had introduced us, though I had leafed through stylish Penguin copies of his novels in bookshops when I was nineteen. At least I had an idea that Martin Amis was out there somewhere. With Bellow I wasn't even sure if he was alive or dead and that seemed somehow disrespectful. It was fine to identify with Shakespeare's turn of phrase, others did, and there was also the protective appearance of times past. Like Bach he was untouchable, immediate, yes, but removed as well. But with Bellow I found myself looking up the publication date in the front. It was written when I was eleven. The blurb said Bellow was born in 1915 in Canada. Nine years older than my father, he'd be eighty-nine this year if he was alive. But even more arresting, on this page was the pencil scribbled $2 which the book had cost me at the university's annual Save the Children Fund book sale. If, at this early stage in the reading of this book, it felt like a whole novel's worth of personal encounter had gone on between me and the author, how strange it was that I had paid two dollars for the privilege! It seemed I would need to keep writing about this experience so that I could keep reading the book. And keep reading so that I could keep writing. Herzog remained strangely undaunted and so must I. There it was: I had found a way out, a possibility to overcome that lethargy in the face of being a writer. I would not stand alongside Bellow, I would let Bellow work on me by reading small sections, big enough to bear. And I would bear them by writing.

When finally I read that last page of *Herzog* and found that his mental state, in the last paragraph, was really no worse than in the opening line, I went away for a few days and, while I was gone, decided I would write Bellow a letter. No, perhaps I'd write it to Herzog – he was the letter-writer, incomplete and rambling though many of his letters had become in his efforts to keep his mind.

IV

Dear Herzog,

 It is to you I write, not Bellow. This is not a writers' con-versation but one between men struggling with the powerful forces of their minds. You have given me courage, Herzog, courage not to yield in spite of terrible internal and external pressures. The normal ones of the complexity of thought, the troubling and jesting acrobatics of emotion, and the intolerable yet seductive grasp of relationship. One of the great merits of your character is that you have all this in you and yet you are a regular person going about your regular activities. If only the regular people who appear on television these days ('cause regular is cool and makes for good TV) had one hundredth of your complexity. The struggle is to maintain some sort of balance between the teeming maelstrom in the brain and the constructed and selected interactions with other people. It's some sort of joke, don't you think, listening to the simplified version of a thought or feeling smoothed out for someone else's consumption. Things need to be palatable, digestible. You can't just go around telling people what you think. The meal is prepared (and I note there are plenty of meals for you in those three hundred pages), first by the selection of ingredients, then the cooking and the addition of a little flavouring. Whatever is in the fridge, whatever is in the cupboard, is not yet fit for consumption. Consumption! That disease of the interface: lungs with air; minds with interactions. The preparation of the meal lies chiefly in the selection of the ingredients. This is the simplification process. It is here that the essence might be defined and it is here that it might be lost.

What a relief, Herzog, to have access to your mind and to feel the companionship, the resonance. Here in Australia we'd call it mateship. Born out of the common struggle faced by two people, here most commonly related to the harshness of the land and the fighting of other nations' wars in distant places. To know that someone out there – Bellow, I guess – has had these struggling thoughts before me is a consolation. How wonderful, Herzog, that you are written down. No waiting for morning to call you. No struggle with Bellow about the translation – what you really meant to say. (Or worse, some university professor – they were so helpful once before – making some point about you.) No, it's just you and me and the consolation that goes with the recognition, the resonance – your thoughts and mine. Sound crazy? Well that's all right with me.

I should tell you that I barely needed the storyline. That was not what appealed, though perhaps it was necessary for Bellow. You and I, fellow participants in the big storyline which lies outside ourselves, outside the individual narrative and keeps us in a conversation beyond the author and the book. 'Course, Bellow had to pin you down, make your portrait, but I liked the way you got your bits of writing in – not much narrative there, just thoughts. As if it were very late at night and the authors had all gone home leaving us to meander on in our conversation about the trouble with it all.

And another thing, Herzog: your mind is described by Bellow. He's your reader, your commentator, your psychotherapist. In the process, I feel he and you have read *me*, offered me some understanding. But there may be a further resonance for me. I gave my $2 copy of the book to my friend Bjorn who just arrived back from Sweden. At our first meeting I introduced the idea.

'Every now and then,' I said, 'I come across a writer who has captured near perfectly what I have been thinking and feeling. And I say to myself, how does this guy know so accurately what's been going on in my head? Know what my inner life is like.'

'What's in your head now?' Bjorn enquired. 'Is this book you're referring to resonant with your inner life now?'

'Yes,' I said and then, a moment's self-consciousness. What if he gets the book and reads it, what will he make of me?

Next time we meet, Bjorn tells me he has gone looking for *Herzog* but has not found a copy.

'After your description I thought I should read it.'

So, a few days later I drop my copy, pencil marks at the top of some pages, in to my friend to read. That's resonance beginning. I have some confidence anyway, 'cause when I first told him about *Herzog* I said: 'I could just get my psychotherapist to read the book!'

And he said: 'You could send her the book and she could send you the bill.'

Now that's the sort of Jewish joke you'd be proud of, Herzog.

Yours,
The Reader

brothers and fathers

... for once, without artifice.

– Martin Amis, *Experience*

I

I always thought our local concert hall was a building people should have more respect for. When the musicians introduced themselves, the composer and the music, I wondered to myself why they never said:

'And ladies and gentlemen, let's turn for a moment to Jeffrey Howlett who, though no longer with us, designed and oversaw the building of this wonderful space where the music can fly up and be contained to resonate a moment for your pleasure.'

I imagined that the crowded heads would look upwards and backwards in reflection at the modernist interior of red and black, the bare concrete walls, and the square shapes which made up the ceiling and concealed the soft air-conditioning that wafted through the auditorium where the music would soon be.

But this did not happen. In fact, the only announcement the night I'm remembering came from a disembodied voice over the public address system advising people to turn off their mobile phones.

The lights faded and the visiting violinist came on to applause from the audience and the other musicians. She was a slight woman barely more than five foot high, with a pointed face and darting shiny eyes which, especially when she moved, gave her an overall appearance of a hamster. The first piece in the program was by a Jewish composer from Czechoslovakia who, the notes explained, had been transported to a concentration camp where he continued composing until he died in January 1945, not much more than a month after his twenty-sixth birthday. The piece was Gideon Klein's *Partita*, arranged for string orchestra by Vojtěch Šádek. Modernist chamber music was not something I warmed to naturally, but as soon as the music began I experienced an intense emotional sympathy for the sounds. They reminded me of something very familiar and I kept trying to think of musical connections to explain this. But none came; it was purely the sound and the colour of the music – its emotions, which made me feel first sympathy towards the music and then a growing sense of sympathy *from* the music. I could remember this same sensation in my teens and early twenties listening to the symphonies of Beethoven and Brahms and later of Mahler and Bruckner. There was the consolation of mirrored emotional experience, part relief, part licence to certain thoughts and feelings. And so it was with the Klein *Partita*, that I felt so at home with this music from someone I had no connection with, had never heard of before that night, that I began to formulate the rather terrible thought that if only my father could have written one piece of music like this – eleven minutes of familiarity – I would have given up the rest of my long relationship with him and resigned myself to him dying in a concentration camp, like Klein, at the age of twenty-six.

Later, my therapist would miss the point and observe: 'Your father never gave you anything of his.'

'No,' I said. 'I would put it differently, he never gave me anything of mine.'

Others had, though, they had been there at the right time with the right capacity to give me something of mine for which I was looking. Take the teacher who, when I was eleven, read to us from a book of Greek myths as well as two poems about horses. How fortunate that our regular sadistic teacher at the time was replaced for a term by a man who gave us Roy Campbell and Banjo Paterson. Fortunate for a boy who loved animals and nature, a boy who would one day move from South Africa to Australia, and fortunate for a boy who needed to locate a sense of the masculine in himself.

My father could not be described as particularly masculine. He was dapper in his presentation and pernickety in his habits. He was also absent a lot of the time. On holidays I watched him. His step was a strange combination of springy upward movement and jarring footfall. He pranced nervously, especially when confronted by nature. On the rocks at the beach he moved as if he were dodging danger. He didn't like putting his head under the water, and when he did, he emerged with a lengthy ritual to rid his face of the contamination. He felt the same about sea-sand. He would reluctantly bare his feet to the beach and walk briskly, lightly sidestepping the incoming waves. At the end of the strand there would be a tedious operation to remove the last grain of sand before the socks and shoes were replaced. (How can the inside of my feet, the flat bit between the ankle and the heel, have the identical feathered blue and violet capillaries as his when so little else is there of him in me?)

I scarcely knew what I was looking at. Yet I had a vague sense of avoidance. I could feel an inclination in myself towards my father's fastidiousness, but being a child allowed me a certain freedom and the obsessive style did not take hold. There were a series of men to watch and to copy: my rugby coach who guided my first efforts at physical endurance; my first father-in-law who was a game ranger and whose comfortable and forceful way of walking through the bush I consciously modelled. They were images of strength to hold up against my father's white-faced, lip-biting violence which occasionally terrified everyone in range. But those men who did offer me the role of the masculine often had a dictatorial stance and they were mostly fleeting presences in my life. On the other hand when I read Joseph Conrad at university he did easily as much for my emerging masculinity as all these men together. Like the Paterson poem, I could read Conrad and make, from the outline he'd drawn, my own version of the man. Heyst and Nostromo and Jim emerged in me. This was not specific instruction; rather, I received their inspiration to be men with their varied capacity for decisions and action.

With the real men in my life, my father included, I watched and tried to include or exclude some of the things which I saw in them but even the smallest item seldom fitted me; they were off-the-rack identities which were ill-fitting or at least needed modification. But the men I encountered in the literature of Conrad, Melville, Kundera, Bellow and Amis were capable of selecting in me already available characteristics. This was not paternal instruction, more a kind of brotherhood situated alongside my experience. It was as if they helped me to find familiar objects of myself – forgotten, unused or not yet recognised. I read at times as if I were studying a picture of myself as a child in a context beyond the reach of memory. Or as if I had picked up, as I have quite often done, something I have written down, usually a dream fragment which I have no memory of at all but there is an essence that is familiar and I notice that the handwriting is mine.

Perhaps the distance in reading ameliorates the narcissism of the author, allowing the reader the freedom to recognise the self. My father never allowed this. There was never any room for my reality outside his version of me which he carried in his head. He would phone me with specific ideas of what I was up to: 'Hello sonny, are you still in bed?' or no salutation at all, just his voice saying:

'You back from walking the dogs? I phoned earlier and you weren't there.' And besides, I was always suspicious of my father's motives. He would often suddenly clarify something which had not been part of any discussion and which often left one feeling dangerously exposed. Like the year we travelled to Europe together after I'd finished school. Arriving at the hotel in London he wanted the large box of tissues which he had asked me if I had room for in my suitcase. I handed it over as I had taken it from him, as if it were the thing it was, something to blow your nose on. But he took the box and turned it over and pried open the glued surfaces of the base. Except for three tissues left at the top of the box for disguise the rest of the box was carefully packed with banknotes I had unwittingly smuggled out of South Africa. These sort of incursions on my growing self were frequent but they never left any marks on me physically and in my shame I never said much about them to anyone else.

Literature was refreshingly upfront with me and I never felt as if it were out to define me at my own cost.

There was scarcely enough time for the Klein *Partita* to drain from the huge space, let alone pool and settle in my psyche, when the visiting violinist, enamoured of the audience approval, was driving the small group of musicians on to the next piece of music. Another Central European and another protest against the same terrible inhumanity. This time it was Karl Amadeus Hartmann's *Concerto Funebre*. Was it the platform of emotional vulnerability which the previous music had set me upon or was it again the recognition of the deep connection to another human being's sense of outraged and terrified grief that led me to an immediate sense of emotional resonance?

I have heard that if the right note is struck intensely enough, a glass might shatter in the same room because of the shared structural frequency. My psyche felt like such a glass as this piece of music emerged from the stage and swirled through the auditorium. The violinist was apparently so moved by the music that her body danced across the stage towards the other violins or back towards the cellos and double bass. Her body doubled over or swayed dangerously backwards as she and her instrument produced the weeping music. Not afforded such physical outlet, my heart raced from the anxiety generated by the agitated notes and then squeezed under my ribs in a thousand tears. Now I could feel the betrayal by all the dangerous fathers and the grief at the life that they kill in their children. The terrifying Goya image of Zeus eating his children was in my mind. And alongside it, the weeping hopelessness of George Frederic Watts' *Hope*, the Victorian painting of the woman, blind and cradling a harp on which a single string still remains intact. But mostly the music was without thought or imagery; I felt only the sharp foreground angst against a constant background of longing and grief.

But how was this thirty year old violinist performing with such fullness of emotional being? What grief had she endured? What gulf of emptiness had she confronted? What horrors of political oppression had she escaped?

How can *she* have this effect on me with this music? Surely it cannot be the music alone? I whispered these last two questions and the answer was wisely: The music knows everything and she is channelling it to us.

II

There are pictures of Martin Amis in *Experience* which help me to visualise him, sitting at a desk, somewhere in London where he lives. He is thinking about his father who is turning his back on the world and on life. But he can glance up to the shelves above the desk and let his eyes play over the volumes that reside there. Collected up to the left, where a person's eyes would go if they were visualising a memory, is a row of books written by Kingsley Amis. This is his father; this is his father's life's work. It is a prodigious oeuvre, one any son might be proud of. An intricate record, an instant access to the mind of the man. The man who, like every father, will one day be gone forever.

I did read Kingsley Amis's *Lucky Jim* once. I didn't find it particularly amusing, though it made me hanker briefly after the structure of belonging which might go with an English education. (Years later, *Engleby* by Sebastian Faulks cast a less attractive and frankly infective light on any lingering romance with such belonging.)

Martin Amis says that his mate Saul Bellow is in communion with him much more than the events of their meetings might suggest. It's because he's on his bookshelves, with other authors, *sleeplessly accessible*. But I've never met Martin Amis. So what is he doing in my house? What difference has he made to me and how

I see the world? Tomorrow my father will call me from New Zealand as he does most Sunday mornings. I face the prospect with a kindness I have only recently been able to muster. My siblings don't validate this kindness. They half think I might be interested in the money. But Amis, who is probably my brother's age, is supportive. He didn't tell me himself, but kindness to one's father, in the face of the unforgivable, twines itself through his narrative, a leitmotif, a kindness motif.

Meanwhile Amis is lying uncomplaining on the lounge room floor where I threw him down earlier this week after finishing the last delicious appendix. It takes courage to finish reading a book like *Experience*; courage to finish writing it too, I imagine – no more to go, nothing more to give. People are not like books: sometimes when they go they go forever. Harold Bloom says one reads because one doesn't have the time in a life to relate to enough people. I turn that around in my mind and place it on its head. Instead I say: *Wouldn't it be wonderful to have a book about every important person in one's life?* They and what they mean to you would be there, next to your bed, in the study, on the kitchen table with patience and unbroken attachment to soothe and contain. Amis is still there for me but some of the best friends of my life are not.

Three months ago I went down the stairs and into the windowless bookshop in a small lane five streets west of my house. Diving below the peopled pavement, I could have been a man setting out on a voyage of discovery as easily as a boy on a ten-minute treasure hunt.

The publishers and booksellers were wrong in their prediction of book-buying behaviour. I didn't choose to read this book because of what was written on the back cover. Nor was it 'cover out' when I found it; it was 'spine out' – evidently a bad selling posture for a book. I had seen the first five pages, heard them read out loud by a woman with a beautiful voice. The influence had begun. I wanted it to continue: I wanted to own a copy of *Experience*. I went straight to where it was on the bookshelves and took down the only copy. It was wedged between another of Martin Amis's and one of his father's. I knew it was what I wanted, and after the transaction, I took it home like a great treasure, a twenty-two dollar treasure.

I reflect now on the relative worth of this *experience*. Let's compare some values here. One of the most valuable things I do in my week is go to see my psychotherapist. The book cost me the same as seven minutes of my psychotherapist's time. At lunchtime today I had a meal in a cafe with my nephew and his girlfriend. My meal and the beer I drank cost a little under the Amis standard and was forgotten by three o'clock. Best we don't get on to friends, where the cost is always in the anxiety about their welfare, the anger at their misunderstanding and the sadness at their sudden departure.

I have felt none of these in relation to the author of *Experience*. Yet the book has told me things I didn't know. It took me by the arm as I lurched along a dangerous mid-life path. And it made me laugh maniacally in the middle of the night. The critic's quote that did appear on the back of the book said the reviewer had been brought to tears three times. They could have said seven hundred laughs and three tears. The tears of mine that blurred the print came from shared recognition; they were not lonely tears. What a gift. And no one much to thank. The pay cheque from the publishers doesn't speak this language. Though I hear Amis quip that fan mail doesn't exactly pay.

It's not the detail or the content which informs me, it's the pattern, the sense, the feeling. Take for example that feeling of responsiveness to the father, which I have always worked hard to maintain. While I could never get up the approbation for my father which Martin Amis shows towards his, I have aspired to the responsiveness. I see Amis grappling unsuccessfully to steady the collapsing bulk of his intoxicated father on the traffic island in Edgware Road. Here is a scene, here is a metaphor, for the son's responsibility to the father. To wrest meaning from the life that is unfolding and fading and to keep responding to it even when, later, the irritable back of the father is turned towards the faithful son.

Cheerfully, always half an eye on the amusement of it all, this 'stranger' has clapped me on the back and said: 'I know what it's like – one just has to keep going so that when the big things happen, and the big things happen to everyone, you're in a place from which you can respond.'

And this fraternal stranger has validated my reading too: *Even the best kind of popular novel just comes straight at you; you have no conversation with a popular novel.* By contrast Amis describes reading a novel of Bellow's as being like a conversation with the author or with Herzog or Henderson or Humboldt. I had a long conversation with Amis, just when I needed to. A whole heap of issues I was facing in my life came up between us. Most memorably the one about what to do with fathers towards the end of their life. I had spent so much time wanting so much more from my father. Amis had a template I could use to think about things. Yes, I could have been envious of what his father had to offer him – for that matter what his brother had to offer him – but this was not the important bit, it was how he continued to *do* a relationship with Kingsley when so many things mitigated against it.

So I played my part, by reading carefully the right book for the time. I took what I needed from the experience and felt gratitude to the author for having done his part. He had written the best book he could, with the conversational spaces which are so hard to define; so subtle and pervasive, one almost wants to call it an attitude. No wonder so much celebrity status attends writing these days and packs out writers festivals with groupies eager to decode the truth from the hand that wrote the novel. You'd expect that kind of reverence in response to a novel that 'came straight at you'; it would be a more passive experience than the hard working conversation I had with Amis.

After the experience, I'm still slightly amazed that buying and reading a book of this significance is not attended by more interpersonal paraphernalia. No exam, no interview, no résumé, no small talk, no selection process whatsoever by the author. His work all done, the rest is up to me. With Amis I read in the first few pages the fascination with the words as they spun out on the page. I heard too a sympathy for the child, the imagination, the unconscious, the missing; those connected items essential to the examined life. And I encountered also in the first pages the intention to examine, in particular, the story of the father and the son: Kingsley and Saul and mine. And all this *without artifice*, but with an onerous complexity, so that he did not write a book called *How to Sustain a Relationship with One's Father – A Son's Manual*. Which of course I wouldn't have read.

I also knew that, in the face of these far from harmless things, Amis intended to be springy and funny. He was treating deadly serious problems with a light touch – *a solemn duty to be cheerful*. This appeals to the man in his late forties who has not had a smooth time of it these last ten years.

The conversation with the author is much like psychotherapy. Figurative, with spaces. I do my job, they make up their lives, develop identities, make things work better. A good writer, explained de Botton, will get us to see our world through his eyes, not just his world through our eyes. The world with another's eyes can liberate.

Amis did this for me where his father never did.

And so the figurative code developed by the artist lies dormant, on the bookshelf, in a gallery, or waiting to be played. Till I, the reader, engage with it. A seed waiting in the dark soil for the water and the sun and the work of life. I sit in the darkened concert hall and find again how great commitment is required to complete this circle. It is no passive activity. If I do the work, Hartmann's gift, like that of the authors, will dignify the capacity of all fathers and all brothers. And in the consolation they offer, my disappointment will be sharpened but my capacity for hope and generativity will be heard, however softly.

the space in the story

There's a crack in everything
That's how the light gets in.
– Leonard Cohen, 'Anthem'

I

When I was a child, books facilitated the relationship between me and my mother. It was a connection, a currency we could both use. Love is something that is given and received. That is why food is such a good symbol of nurture; it is provided, but to be meaningful it must be taken in. My mother read to me and via that other person – the character in the story or the author – I took in an emotional connection. Some triangles are less toxic than others, some are very useful indeed.

Later, I learnt about life from books but I also learnt

about myself from them. From entering the characters of the novels I read, I discovered what sort of person I was and what sort of person I might become. I played a more and more conscious part in this process. At first I used the university syllabus to guide my choice. In time, with some authors like Lawrence and Conrad and Kundera, I developed a relationship with the author as I came to realise that the themes they were addressing were those with which I needed more rehearsal. Conrad could tell me about principles and manhood and steadfast commitment and their counterparts, weakness and failure. With Lawrence's help I could figure out how this manhood was to be negotiated in relation to women. Kundera, in turn, could relate both these masculine themes to an understanding of politically repressive regimes.

Later still, in adulthood, I learnt how to find a book that was going to be good for me. Principally I learnt about the authenticity of the author and the Greek derivation of these two words. At first I didn't know I was doing this, but I could gauge the self of an author and their likely relationship to the self of me. I could pick up a book in a library or bookshop and with some confidence turn to somewhere towards the middle and read a page or so. I would go for dense text, not dialogue, for a medium-length paragraph, not a long or short one, and not something at the beginning or end of a chapter. Somewhere, encoded in the language I read there, I would find the markers I was looking for, a sort of coherence, a pattern that would tell me something about the author. It was like testing the DNA of the writer, a thumb print which would tell me whether or not I wanted to read the book.

As with people, there were books in the middle of this scale which I would find hard to assess. But, with some reliability and speed, I would find books that I did not want to read and books that I did want to read. This worked for me and was necessary, given my slow reading pace, and the time constraints that put on this precious occupation. I never thought I was inventing a method of finding books that would be suitable for other people to read. This was not a tool for the foundational assessment of good literature, more a method of selecting the books and the authors which would suit my reading needs.

How does one select one's friends? One's lovers? One's psychotherapists? At the outset I was uncertain of who I was and had to rely on the judgement of others and on the luck of circumstance. Later, with the aid of fellow travellers chanced upon, I developed a clearer sense of myself. This solid core allowed me to see the world more clearly and to become more reliable in the selection of others. To no longer bend the interpersonal space with a strangeness unknown to myself. To take a reliable photograph one has to hold the camera still. But one learns to do this in time. And if, from one's early experience, all one has is a poorly focused view of a person one loved, one will treasure the gloss-worn print as if it were part of one's identity.

Reading in my adult life became a little less driven for me. In adolescence I read as if my life depended on it, and I think it did. Then, increasingly, I read for enjoyment rather than for survival. With that, I became better at selecting the books which were going to be meaningful to me. I became a more efficient reader. And finally, the continuing development of this process was in becoming a writer. As I repeatedly heard my own voice in the writing of others, I began to distinguish what might be unique in that voice of mine. Writing teachers have the truism: 'There is a story only you can tell'. Perhaps when one has read and read, read with care and dedication and commitment, read with a purpose, one might begin to hear a writing voice that is only one's own to use.

But what people have read is so inflated in discussion, that the influence of what they have really read is sometimes deflated. At one time, I went around asking people what three books were most important to them in their life so far. At first some didn't understand what I was getting at and I would have to refine the question to: 'What do you think would be the three books that have had the most influence on who you are?' That question itself would surprise people and alert them, some, apparently for the first time, to the importance I was attaching to literature. A number of books came up in several people's selection, but mostly I was struck by the diversity of the books that people listed. Hardly any of the books were on my list.

It's surprising how often people say they've read a book when they haven't. One would be much less likely to say that one has met a certain person when one hasn't, than to say one has read a book one hasn't. Perhaps one should rather ask: Do you have a relationship with such and such a book? Because many people who have read the book may not have developed a relationship with it and some people who have not read the book may, nevertheless, have a relationship with it.

This has happened a lot to me in my consulting room as a psychotherapist. Often, when a book or an author has been very important to someone it will emerge in the psychotherapy. Sometimes I have read the book and this puts a particular degree of difficulty on things since we will have to first establish that our appreciation has been similar or different with all the feelings of connection or disconnection which come with that. So, in a way it is preferable if I, as psychotherapist, have not read the important book or met the important person. That way the importance of the relationship and its meaning can be left with the client. The narrative or metaphors or the meaning or the unfolding relationship contained within the book are then presented by the client, often with some emotional power, since the influence has been profound. Later, in another session, with another client, this metaphor or narrative may seem to me to be important and I'll ask whether the person has read the book that has been previously discussed with me. I might say: 'Well I haven't, but I have it second-hand from another client of mine and there is a part of it which seems particularly apt to what you are describing.' Then I'll go ahead and quote it and, for a time, the book may become meaningful again in the discussion of two people who haven't read it.

I know also of books that have been important to people before they read them and also of books that have been important to people though they've never read them. *Doctor Zhivago* is my favourite personal example of that. At fourteen, when I first saw the film, it was too difficult for me to read the dense text, though I tried in vain. The book remains on my list of things to read, while the film, which I have seen several times since, remains a centrally important item to my psychological life. But think also of the bookshelves in the house where you grew up. My partner Rebecca says she knew that The Russians were over in one section of her parents' bookcase and that sometime later she would get to them. I felt like that about the five Somerset Maughams, especially the thick one with the provocative title *Of Human Bondage* which sat on my brother's planks-and-bricks bookshelves in our family home and which beckoned to me somewhere in the future. I never did find resonance with that author. Dickens, on the other hand – who first I thrilled to at thirteen, when an English teacher read the class *A Tale of Two Cities* – lay waiting for me until, in adulthood, I was able to tackle such large books myself. I found shelves in the library to be like places on a map; they promised something which, even without venturing there, stimulated the imagination. In my atlas I could imagine with internal clarity what the land would be like as my finger traced the continent of South America or the island of Borneo. I did the same with the likes of Chaucer, James, the federation of Brontës and Bellow, tracing their outline in my mind before ever reading them. And I was provoked into still more exotic thoughts by Dostoyevsky, Proust and Cervantes.

There are books one may not have read, which, nevertheless, are so well known that, as one goes along one develops an idea of what they are like, even what they are about. *War and Peace* and *Don Quixote* must be towards the top of this list for many English speakers. But my personal favourite example is Mark Twain's *Adventures of Huckleberry Finn*. This book has occupied a place in my imagination for many years, yet only recently did I read it. I found there were peculiarities in the story which did not fit with my version. Jim and Huck spent a lot more time actually navigating the Mississippi than I had imagined; and I had not realised that they were on the run, more than they were just out there on an adventure for the sake of it. There was not as much detail in the fishing or getting of vittles as I'd thought appropriate for this novel; and there were no encounters with beavers at all. I think I'd imagined that Tom Sawyer, and some of the other boys, were along for the ride from the beginning. And I had no idea of the ever-present danger of Jim being apprehended as a runaway slave. I had imagined him to be Huck's age – two boys exploring the river together in a kind of endless holiday. Mark Twain wanted more from me, and it's possible he would have got more if I'd read the book in South Africa when I was fifteen. I would have questioned the racism of the Southern countryside in a way which could have enlightened me as to my own political circumstances more rapidly than the slow dawning which did occur.

II

Richard comes to see me and we realise it's been fifteen years we've had these monthly discussions, this psychotherapy. I used to think of him as the man who lost his mother when he was five. He used to introduce himself that way; somewhere within the first few paragraphs of meeting somebody new, he'd say: 'Ah but you see that's where you and I are different, I lost my mother when I was five.' The experience had somehow bent him out of shape; like a backbone with a twenty-degree sideways bend in it. Later, when he was old enough, the shape he invented for himself built in the differences between him and other people even more. Like light rays through water, the connections he made with other people were refracted – twenty degrees off.

For the first years of our meetings, we talked about the loss of his mother and all the things that resulted from it. Like his failure at school and the interruption of his great talent for art, and how difficult it had been for him to understand socialising and relationships. From my point of view, a breakthrough came one day when I asked him an important question. 'What were things like for you *before* your mother died?' That question lay outside his usual account of things. For a moment it seemed I might have said something terribly inappropriate. There was a sort of disorientation in him as he gathered together an answer. He trusted that I knew him well enough that an answer wouldn't destroy the main story of his life. He told me he could remember a warm and loving presence that was his mother. As he talked of her I could see a space open up in him. Light through a previously unseen crack. From that afternoon I stopped thinking of him as the man whose mother died when he was five, and a small flexibility grew in our usually stiff conversation.

Today we talk about his mother again. We haven't

referred much to her in the last year or two. He's gradually been thinking of other things: his work and the awkward and sometimes neglected relationships with his family and the world. Recently he's been wanting to write about his experiences and so he talks about how he might portray his mother and the terrible loss in a way that others would understand.

'I came down the stairs when I woke one morning and someone told me my mother had died; gone; dead in the night. At first I couldn't understand the words they were saying but then very slowly the words got in and started to mean something; started to hurt. From that moment on my life changed completely.'

Then he paused and the next thing he said was new to our conversation, probably new to his thinking: 'It was my mother's death that night and then, the small chain of circumstances which followed, that changed my life completely. Things happened around me which seemed to stop me from responding in any other way than I have. A spell was cast on me and only recently has the malady started to be dispelled.'

I thought of the spaces in the story. When Richard first came to see me, he began to open up the space between the events long ago and his memory of them. He could stop remembering himself *as* the death of his mother and start thinking of himself as the person to whom the tragedy had occurred. Relived events became narrated experience. Then, years into our discussion, came this space he'd just opened up, between the event of his mother's death and the small chain of circumstances which followed it. He was right, these together had cemented his response into an inflexible development in his personality and he'd gone on responding to the world in the same way for the next forty years. Now he was writing about those events and yet another space was opening up in him.

The spaces in the story are the places where some light and movement can get in. The spaces show themselves when the story gets told *and* is properly listened to. And in the fertile ground of these spaces figurative language grows and with it, movement forwards can begin again.

When it comes to making spaces, writing is one of those precious activities. I'd felt the spaces when I started writing myself onto the page. I lived on my own with my dog. I was in the middle of my life and things needed revisioning. I would write every Friday night until two or three in the morning. If I were out in the evening, I would nurse the anticipation of writing like a pleasurable secret and excuse myself from the gathering at ten and hurry home to play Sarah Brightman's voice at one end of the house and unfold my laptop at the other end. Fergus would curl up at my feet and we wouldn't move for hours. But I was moving. The writing spun out onto the screen and as it did so I felt liberated. Liberated by the space opening up between what was in my head, the memory of things long past, and the words on the page.

Writers have sometimes referred to this helpful, almost healing space. It does its magic by prying open cracks in the story, levering some flexibility in the self – a sort of psychological yoga. I've heard Detective Inspector Rebus's creator, Ian Rankin, say how important his character is to him. Rebus can do all the things that society or his relationships don't allow Rankin to do, like go and kill someone in a car crash because they swore at him in the park. That's a space, a big and obvious one, for the writer. The more subtle one is the turning of a memory, one sort of thought stuck in one's head, into a narrative with words and punctuation. Out on the page the event still happened but now it's not exactly the same, something has been lost, something has been gained.

Psychotherapy is like that, it opens up a space. Sometimes stories that have never been put into words emerge in the listening space between one and the other. The other is the psychotherapist, he is the reader; the patient is the writer. Sometimes of course these told stories get stuck not as original memories but as stuck stories themselves, ones that have never been listened to closely enough to get the light of difference in.

What if there is no one to read you, when you need it most? To keep you from getting set in the hardening quagmire of the past? How might a person keep moving through the events of their life so as not to petrify? Might it be that reading itself can put the life back in: open a small space; allow for a reflection from what is read to the life that needs to be read? This would explain why only some books, at some stages in the life, affect one so deeply as to change the nature of who one is. That is why they shape the development of one's identity, they limber up a little reflective space between one's own experience and those of the narrator. They can provide another person's language for an experience one has had. The writer *reads* the reader so the reader can keep moving on. This is more than consolation. It is an opportunity to recast the self so that a different story might emerge, a different life than might have been expected from the early settings.

F. Scott Fitzgerald's novel *The Great Gatsby* ends with the line: *So we beat on, boats against the current, borne back ceaselessly into the past.* Take the space between me and F. Scott Fitzgerald. Or is it more correctly between me and how Fitzgerald portrayed Gatsby? I receive that metaphor of the boats beating on against the current as he intended, but because it is a metaphor I am free to interpret it personally – this too is space. I know that I am more optimistic about life than he is, at least than he is for his main character. I know that as I and others are borne back ceaselessly into the past in my consulting room and as we *together* light up spaces in the story, that our characters are changed, liberated by the action, renewed.

There are two major differences between Richard's experience and my own. The first is that the trauma he suffered was sudden, physical, and to the boy of five, life-threatening. This last made the cement between the event and the ensuing interpersonal events even more solid. My trauma – it should almost be called by a different name – was interpersonal trauma, what psychologists call *developmental trauma*. Things went wrong between me and the people who were caring for me, those to whom I was attached. It was only the 'small chain of interpersonal events' which disrupted my growing up. This meant that the connection between my experience and the interpersonal events was not so solid, other experiences and other people could come in and help flex my growing self. Some of these people and experiences were the characters in the books that I read.

The second major difference between Richard's experience and mine was that he didn't read. Perhaps he didn't have the space between the self and the interpersonal world to allow him to; perhaps he didn't have the educational help; but more than those, he no longer had a mother, as I did, to read *to* him. I did have the mother to read to me and that experience led me, later, to read myself.

The writer, like the psychotherapist, may help the reader, his unknown client. But the writer is helped by this process too. The same spaces which the writer benefits from in her story will be the spaces where the reader can grow themselves and a conversation can take place. Just so, the psychotherapist can benefit from the process of the psychotherapy he does with his clients. We are that similar. All our stories seem so different but, when the patterns are felt and understood, they are the same.

When we go into a library or a bookshop with intent, we sometimes have the lucky experience of selecting a book, a writer, who, because we have chosen their writing well, will, because they have written well, listen very closely to us and we will be changed forever.

I now swim more confidently in the library which used to feel like deep and turbulent water. Though I am still a hesitant reader, literature has become the commodity which saved me. Nurturing me through long and hopeless days of childhood where others could not console me. Forming me to be more like myself in my strange youth which thus became less strange to me. Yet made me more a stranger in my own land. And in adulthood, synthesising the consolation and identity into a path towards the future – one of those magical scribbled moon-paths on the ocean at night – always the same, always different.

coda

Somewhere, everywhere, now hidden, now apparent in whatever is written down is the form of a human being.
— Virginia Woolf, 'Reading'

I

She is with me still, Virginia Woolf, as Shakespeare's sister famously was with her. I've not read all her books, not a tenth of her letters and diaries, not a third of her essays and yet I know she thinks something very similar to me about the activity of reading, and that makes her a literary friend forever.

Drowned? Even as I came to the end of writing these essays I dived into the library one day and came up with more of her to relate to. I had imagined that I would call my collection of personal reflections *Reading*. The simplicity of the title appealed to me. Then from *The Common Reader* I found her essay entitled 'Reading'. Hers is a kind of homage to history and to the men and women who had priorities other than writing – ploughing, fighting, exploring. Back then, when things needed to be written, there were simple accounts unburdened with emotion; and yet how all of this made reading possible for us, preparing the place where we may sit and read by a window. Then later there came the writers in a long avenue which, from the present, one might look down *hosts of them merging in the mass of Shakespeare* ... And how Sir Thomas Browne seems to her to bring in for the first time: ... *the whole question, which is afterwards to become of such importance, of knowing one's author*. And here *I* sit and think I know again *my* author and not only that, but what she thought and felt about reading – my subject.

Take, as an example, her reverie while reading:

> ... *somehow or another, the windows being open, and the book held so that it rested upon a background of excalonia hedges and distant blue, instead of being a book it seemed as if what I read was laid upon the landscape, not printed, bound, or sewn up, but somehow the product of trees and fields and the hot summer sky, like the air which swam, on fine mornings round the outlines of things.*

I too have felt the slightly crazy sense of the continuity of what I am reading with the reality of what the writing is about. Life swimming about the meta-reality of the written word. I too have held up a book against the background, this time of eucalypts and casuarinas. But I have more commonly held up a book against the background of emotions and relationships and actions, and the merging continuities and border discrepancies have challenged and validated me.

But as soon as I feel I have found something of Virginia, I am suspicious of myself and must back away. I must retreat to her novels. Even in the essay on reading she has a warning, flighted as usual in enchanting metaphor, that one might kill the beauty by capturing it, by trying to know it and own it like a prize moth with scarlet underwings captured and killed in the night forest.

Last week I met an author who studied the work of her favourite poet until she finished her PhD. Now she can't face that poetry any more, can't stand the stuff. A poet and her writing killed, at least for that reader, by a PhD. It is the literature itself which is lively. On the other hand, there is some writing, though meaning to be literature, which seems already captured and pinned to a display board; the words, in spite of being perfectly arranged, have the juice all sucked out of them. No space, no relationship, no life. No capacity to change you forever.

Yet sometimes only the source will do and my affinity with the author is strong, the relationship between us seems entirely personal; it is there in Virginia's feeling for the great mass of writing which was not unlike the feeling I had when at first I couldn't read and later I felt so much was there to read that I might drown in it all:

The books gently swelled neath my hand as I drew it across them in the dark. Travels, histories, memoirs, the fruit of innumerable lives. The dusk was brown with them. Even the hand thus sliding seemed to feel beneath its palm fullness and ripeness. Standing at the window and looking out into the garden, the lives of all these books filled the room behind with a soft murmur. Truly, a deep sea, the past, a tide which will overtake and overflow us.

II

A few months ago I found myself worrying that my analyst Gloria may soon die and I would have no further access to her. This though it is certainly over thirty years since my last session with her and probably twenty-five since last we communicated with each other. Late one Friday night, on a whim, I phoned a friend in South Africa where it would be mid-afternoon and asked him if he had Gloria's telephone number. Yes he had, but he added doubtfully that she was not much in communication with people these days; perhaps it was that she had recently been unwell. I didn't wait for any doubts to crowd my resolution but immediately dialled her number. She answered. I said who it was and was preparing to say that she may not remember her patient from a long time ago who had left and gone to live in Australia. But more than my name was not necessary, there wasn't even a pause, no scrabbling through her memory, she just said: 'Oh hello, how are you?' She said it as if our last appointment had been a fortnight ago, perhaps I'd missed a couple of sessions or been away somewhere for a week or two. We talked on for an hour or so, on equal terms and very much in the present, her family and mine, what life was like for each of us, and how she was preparing to die.

Then one Saturday morning I ran into Rodney in town and we leaned up against a four-wheel drive vehicle and talked about life in the way that one sometimes can, impromptu, a window open for a brief time between two people who don't know each other very well. I complained briefly about the need for a writer to consider the public, not one's reader, but the public who are going to decide about the popularity of one's writing.

'I won't have my writing teacher telling me to remember that my public are middle-aged women who discuss books with others while drinking wine and eating cake. I won't put a Frenchman in the story just for them. I don't earn my keep this way, so I can still be high-minded about writing if I want to. I don't care about the public, I only care about my reader.'

'Quite right too,' Rodney said. And then he told me a story.

'Years ago I took myself off to Florence. I needed to sniff the Renaissance again. But unexpectedly for that time and place there was a Henry Moore exhibition. I got Kenneth Clark's book about him and I went to take a look. Up three flights of steps, with my book. One landing, then another, and there right outside the exhibition, I looked up the last few stairs into the eyes, the liveliest, most beautiful blue eyes of a large man. It was Henry Moore. I hadn't realised how like my father he was. He smiled engagingly and said how nice to see me. And I said how delightful it was to see him conjured up in the space between me and my book about him and the exhibition. We got into a conversation and I asked him: 'Apart from the cash, what's in all this for you?' He smiled and was thoughtful and then he said: 'I do this simply to distract the eye.'

The last paragraph of Virginia's essay on reading also approaches this

> *doubtful region – the region of beauty ... perhaps one of the invariable properties of beauty is that it leaves in the mind a desire to impart. Some offering we must make; some act we must dedicate, if only to move across the room and turn the rose in the jar, which, by the way, has dropped its petals.*

Driving home from my chance encounter with Rodney who I barely know, I thought of Gloria and the region of beauty – an act of dedication. After the phone conversation with her it wasn't what we had said to each other that was so striking to me but that there had been that space in our minds for each other preserved over the long years of being apart. Like a book which may not have been opened for twenty years but which retains its place on the shelf of books that are closest to my heart.

sources

epigraph

Page IV 'For the desire to read ...', Virginia Woolf, 'Sir Thomas Browne', *The Essays of Virginia Woolf Vol. III*, Hogarth Press, London, 1988, p.368.

Page IV 'I see Bellow perhaps twice a year ...', Martin Amis, *Experience*, Vintage, London, 2001, p.268.

prelude

Page 3 'In the beginning God created ...', Genesis 1:1.

Page 3 'In the beginning was the Word ...', ibid., John 1:1.

Page 5 'Why come to life again?', D.H. Lawrence, *Women in Love*, Penguin, 1980, p.206.

Page 7 When I read Martin Amis' autobiographical account ..., Martin Amis, *Experience*, Vintage, 2001.

Page 8   When I read *The Joke* ..., Milan Kundera, *The Joke*, Penguin, 1982, p. xii.

Page 8   She would need no reward in heaven ..., Virginia Woolf, 'How Should One Read a Book?' in *The Common Reader*, Hogarth Press, London 1935, p.270.

Page 9   Was there insufficient salve for her despair in Wordsworth ..., Virginia Woolf, *The Diary of Virginia Woolf*. Vol. V 1936–1941, Hogarth Press, London, 1984, p.295.

the stolen child

Page 10   'Come away, O human child!', W.B. Yeats, 'The Stolen Child', *Collected Poems of W.B. Yeats*, Macmillan, London, 1971, p.20.

Page 13   'It's you, it's you must go and I must bide', 'Danny Boy', Frederic Edward Weatherly, 1913.

Page 19   '"Look! Look! The Princess! Be she going away?"', Paul Gallico, *The Snow Goose*, Penguin, London, 1967, p.22.

sally and miriam

Page 21   'When we are young, and read most passionately ...', Harold Bloom, *How to Read and Why*, Fourth Estate, London, 2000, p.197.

Page 25   'One day in March he lay on the bank of Nethermere ...', D.H. Lawrence, *Sons and Lovers*, Penguin, London, 1969, p.239.

Page 26   'She had scornful grey eyes ...', ibid., p.228.

shopping with clara

Page 30   '"Where should we go for dinner?"', ibid., p.122.

Page 35   '"Now, just look at that fuchsia!"', ibid., p.124.

reading and writing

Page 39   'apartheid ... slum ... township', *The Concise Oxford Dictionary*, Oxford University Press, London, 1964.

intermezzo

Page 50   'authentic', ibid.

Page 54   'Athos's stories gradually veered me from my past', Anne Michaels, *Fugitive Pieces*, Vintage, New York, 1998, p.28.

Page 55   'If we shadows have offended ...', William Shakespeare, *A Midsummer Night's Dream*, V. Epilogue (1), *The Norton Shakespeare*, London, 1997.

Page 57   'Writing when properly managed ...', Laurence Sterne, *The Life and Opinions of Tristram Shandy*, Penguin, London, 1972, p.127.

ignoring icarus

Page 62   'The youth in vain his melting pinions shakes', Ovid, 'The Story of Daedalus and Icarus', *Metamorphoses*, VIII:183–235, trans. Sir Samuel Garth, John Dryden et al., *The Internet Classics Archive*, 1994.

Page 66   'About suffering they were never wrong', W.H. Auden, 'Musée des Beaux Arts', *W.H. Auden: Poems Selected by John Fuller*, Faber, London, 2000, p.29.

Page 67   'In Breughel's Icarus, for instance ...', ibid.

did you read *doctor zhivago?*

Page 71   'For poetry makes nothing happen ...', 'In Memory of W.B. Yeats', ibid., p.33.

hamlet

Page 87   'The prince prophesies our limits ...', Harold Bloom, op. cit., p.217.

Page 90   ... what Bloom refers to as 'self-overhearing', ibid., p.205.

Page 90   '... everyone he speaks to in the play ...', ibid., p.207.

Page 91   'Imagine that you are one of these ...', ibid., p.207.

Page 99   'the native hue ...', William Shakespeare, *Hamlet*, III.i.84–85, *The Arden Shakespeare Hamlet*, Routledge, London, 1982, p.280.

Page 100   'What's Hecuba to him ...', ibid., II.ii.553–560, p.270.
Page 100   'This is I, Hamlet the Dane', ibid., V.i.250–251, p.391.
Page 101   the 'secular scripture', Harold Bloom, *The Western Canon. The Books and School of the Ages*, Harcourt, Orlando, 1993, p.24.
Page 101   'There are more things in heaven and earth, Horatio ...', William Shakespeare, op. cit., I.v.174–175, p.226.

my mother's book

Page 102   'Those who know ghosts tell us ...', Hans Loewald, *Papers on Psychoanalysis*, Yale University Press, New Haven, 1980, p.249.

being herzog

Page 114   'Not that long disease, my life ...', Saul Bellow, *Herzog*, Penguin, New York, 1984, p.10.
Page 115   '... he admitted that he had been a bad husband – twice...', ibid., p.10–11.
Page 117   'No, I've had all the psychiatry I can use.', ibid., p.19.
Page 117   'If I am out of my mind ...', ibid., p. 7.
Page 118   'Call me Ishmael', Herman Melville, *Moby-Dick*, Wordsworth Classics, London, 1993, p.3.
Page 122   'You must aim the imagination also at yourself ...', Saul Bellow, op.cit., p. 124.

Page 125   'The strength of Herzog's constitution ...', ibid., p.18.
Page 126   'In his posture of collapse ...', ibid., p.17.
Page 126   '... his arms rising behind him ...', ibid., p.11.
Page 126   'Not everyone threatened with a crackup ...', ibid., p.13.
Page 126   'Indignation is so wearing ...', ibid., p.17.
Page 126   'He had been hoping ...', ibid., p.19.

brothers and fathers

Page 132   '...for once, without artifice ...', Martin Amis, *Experience*, Vintage, London, 2001, p.7.
Page 139   '... sleeplessly accessible ...', ibid., p.268.
Page 142   'Even the best kind of popular novel ...', ibid., p.224
Page 144   '... a solemn duty to be cheerful', ibid., p.94
Page 144   A good writer, explained de Botton ..., *How Proust Can Change Your Life,* Alain de Botton, Pantheon Books, New York. 1997, p.196.

the space in the story

Page 146   'There's a crack in everything ...', Leonard Cohen, 'Anthem', *The Future*, Columbia Records, 1993.
Page 157   'So we beat on, boats against the current ...', F. Scott Fitzgerald, *The Great Gatsby*, Macmillan, New York, 1992, p.189.

coda

Page 160   'Somewhere, everywhere, now hidden ...', Virginia Woolf, 'Reading', *Collected Essays Vol.II,* Hogarth Press, London, 1966, p.29.
Page 161   '... hosts of them merging ...', ibid., p.13.
Page 161   '... the whole question ...', ibid., p.29.
Page 161   '... somehow or another, the windows being open ...', ibid., p.13.
Page 162   'The books gently swelled neath my hand ...', ibid., p.22.
Page 165   '... doubtful region – the region of beauty', ibid., p.33.

acknowledgements

Personal thanks to Bjorn Lundin for his exquisite reading and suggestions; to Phillip Adams who encouraged me so generously; to Georgia Richter for her editorial alchemy; and to Rebecca Adams – my number one reader. Thanks too to Genevieve Hawks for her excellent administrative assistance.

The author gratefully acknowledges permission to quote from the following: *Experience,* copyright © Martin Amis, published by Jonathan Cape. Reprinted by permission of The Random House Group Ltd; 'Musée des Beaux Arts' and 'In Memory of W.B. Yeats', copyright © 1976, 1991, The Estate of W.H. Auden; *Herzog*: copyright © 1961, 1963, 1964, The Estate of Saul Bellow. Copyright renewed © 1989, 1991, 1992, The Estate of Saul Bellow. All rights reserved; 'Anthem', Excerpt from 'Anthem' from *Stranger Music: Selected Poems and Songs* by Leonard Cohen © 1993. Reprinted with permission. All rights reserved; *The Great Gatsby,* copyright © F. Scott Fitzgerald, Macmillan, 1992; *The Snow Goose,* copyright © Paul Gallico, first published by Michael Joseph; *Papers on Psychoanalysis,* copyright © Hans Loewald, Yale University Press; *Fugitive Pieces,* copyright © Anne Michaels, Vintage and Bloomsbury, 1996. All rights reserved.

First published 2012 by
FREMANTLE PRESS
25 Quarry Street, Fremantle 6160
(PO Box 158, North Fremantle 6159)
Western Australia
www.fremantlepress.com.au

Copyright © Andrew Relph, 2012

The moral rights of the author have been asserted.

This book is copyright. Apart from any fair dealing for the purpose of private study, research, criticism or review, as permitted under the Copyright Act, no part may be reproduced by any process without written permission. Enquiries should be made to the publisher.

Consultant editor Georgia Richter
Cover design Tracey Gibbs
Cover photograph © Don Bayley

 A catalogue record for this book is available from the National Library of Australia

ISBN 9781921696800 (paperback)

Fremantle Press is supported by the Western Australian State Government through the Department of Cultural Industries, Tourism and Sport.

Publication of this title was assisted by the Commonwealth Government through Creative Australia, its arts funding and advisory body.

www.ingramcontent.com/pod-product-compliance
Lightning Source LLC
Chambersburg PA
CBHW020331170426
43200CB00006B/352